Surface Appliqué for Quilting

SURFACE APPLIQUÉ
FOR QUILTING

SUSAN M. COTTRELL

STERLING PUBLISHING CO., INC. NEW YORK
A STERLING/CHAPELLE BOOK

Chapelle, Ltd., Inc.,
P.O. Box 9252, Ogden, UT 84409
(801) 621-2777 • (801) 621-2788 Fax
e-mail: chapelle@chapelleltd.com
Web site: chapelleltd.com

The written instructions, photographs, designs, patterns, and projects in this volume are intended for the personal use of the reader and may be reproduced for that purpose only. Any other use, especially commercial use, is forbidden under law without the written permission of the copyright holder.

Every effort has been made to ensure that all information in this book is accurate. However, due to differing conditions, tools, and individual skills, the publisher cannot be responsible for any injuries, losses, and/or other damages which may result from the use of the information in this book.

Due to the limited amount of space available, we must print our patterns at a reduced size in order to give our patrons the maximum number of patterns possible in our publications. We believe the quality and quantity of our patterns will compensate for any inconvenience this may cause.

Library of Congress Cataloging-in-Publication Data

Cottrell, Susan M.
    Surface appliqué for quilting / Susan M. Cottrell.
        p.cm.
    "A Sterling/Chapelle book."
    Includes index.
    ISBN 1-4027-2001-7
    1. Applqiué–Patterns. 2. Quilting. 3. Fancy work. I. Title.

    TT779.C68 2005
    746.44'5041–dc22   2005008773
10 9 8 7 6 5 4 3 2 1

Published by Sterling Publishing Co., Inc.
387 Park Avenue South, New York, NY 10016
©2005 by Susan M. Cottrell
Distributed in Canada by Sterling Publishing
⅟ Manda Group, 165 Dufferin Street
Toronto, Ontario, Canada M6K 3H6
Distributed in Great Britain by Chrysalis Books Group PLC,
The Chrysalis Building, Bramley Road, London W10 6SP, England
Distributed in Australia by Capricorn Link (Australia) Pty. Ltd.
P.O. Box 704, Windsor, NSW 2756, Australia
Printed in China
All Rights Reserved

Sterling ISBN 1-4027-2001-7

For information about custom editions, special sales, premium and corporate purchases, please contact Sterling Special Sales Department at 800-805-5489 or specialsales@sterlingpub.com.

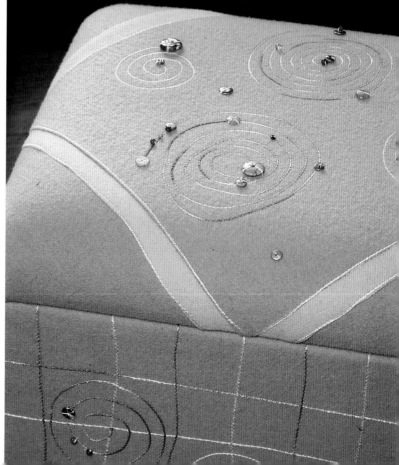

TABLE OF CONTENTS

INTRODUCTION

I have never been successful in resisting beautiful threads, yarns, and cords that have delicious colors and textures. Beads of all shapes and sizes; brass trinkets in any form; splendid wools, old and new; these are things I cannot walk past without handling and inevitably purchasing. These fascinating finds should not sit unused forever. The question is, "What do I do with all these treasures other than take them out once in a while and stare?" I am certain that I am not alone with this wonderful frustration.

In my mind, I see paintings, pillows, wall hangings, and lots of other stuff. In this book, I want to share with you some of my creations. I would like to inspire you to find a great design to use with your treasures. Consider textures and colors in the things that you have, combinations you can create with a streak of this and a snip of that, adding threads to simulate bark, veins in a leaf, stones in a path, a starry night. What about all those scraps of copper and tin, little embellishments found in the craft stores that are to be used for one thing but you think would work on something else?

In this book the technique of appliqué is used a great deal. It is perhaps not the typical appliqué that one thinks of on beautiful quilts and clothing but it is a form of appliqué. Appliqué is one of the simplest and oldest ways to decorate cloth. Like patchwork appliqué was originally used to cover worn or damaged areas in a garment or other useful item. The sewer became clever in turning a disadvantage into an ornamental accent very quickly, thus the art of appliqué began.

THE QUESTION IS, "WHAT DO I DO WITH ALL THESE TREASURES OTHER THAN TAKE THEM OUT ONCE IN A WHILE AND STARE?"

CONSIDER TEXTURES AND COLORS IN THE
THINGS THAT YOU HAVE, COMBINATIONS
YOU CAN CREATE WITH A STREAK OF THIS
AND A SNIP OF THAT, ADDING THREADS
TO SIMULATE BARK, VEINS IN A LEAF,
STONES IN A PATH, A STARRY NIGHT.

The variety of fabrics, textures, and colors that one can use
when appliquéing is so exciting—there are no limits to what you
can do. In this book we will explore a variety of ways to apply
our fabric designs. Machine sewing, using as many of the decorative stitches available there, both complicated and simple will
give you many options. Hand-sewing will allow you to choose
from the unlimited variety of beautiful designs found in embroidery. Gluing will allow a quick and easy way to finish a project.
Using these methods separately or in combination can only lead
to a successful project.

Consider this book a springboard to explore and expand
you creativity. Materials, stitches, and embellishments used in this
book are merely a guide. Do not hesitate to make alterations.
The possibilities are endless. If you do not like hand-sewing,
use a sewing machine. If you do not like to sew, there are lots
of alternatives: very effective glues and adhesives. Just open up
your mind and see where your creativity takes you.

GENERAL ITEMS

Following are materials and tools to have on hand before beginning each project, along with the required materials list for each project:

- Assorted needles
- Assorted threads
- Craft scissors
- Fabric glue
- Fabric shears
- Fray preventative
- Pencil
- Photocopier
- Sewing machine
- Sewing-machine needles
- Straight pins
- Tape measure
- Tracing paper (optional)
- Cording foot, regular foot, zipper foot attachments for sewing machine
- Washable fabric marker

Wool Heart Pillow on page 69

GENERAL INFORMATION

Before beginning to create the projects in this book, please familiarize yourself with general information below and try to remember that you will be enjoying your work longer than it took to create it. Take care to correct mistakes and adjust things so that they will be done as well as possible; however, perfection is not always possible or desirable. This is a difficult line to walk; you will see in most of the projects that there is a lot of latitude in the design and technique. Decide how much effort a project is worth, then put that effort into it. Have fun and enjoy yourself, that is the most important thing to remember.

Wools

This book uses a lot of beautiful wools, all of which have been felted. That is, washed in very hot water with a tablespoon of detergent and dried in a hot dryer. This can be repeated several times. The wool comes out shrunken and thicker; it tends to not fray and has such a great feel (touch) to it. (Photo 1)

Photo 1

Adhesives

A vital part of any craft is the ability to hold the craft project together. Craft glues, fabric glue, and adhesive strips intended to hold a tennis racquet grip in place, are used in this book. Additionally, there are wonderful fusible interfacings, fusible webbing, and iron-on adhesive tapes that can add body and are great for holding your work together. Fray preventive and fabric stabilizer are useful items to have when using glues. Use a glue that you are comfortable working with and that will securely hold the intended item(s). (Photo 2)

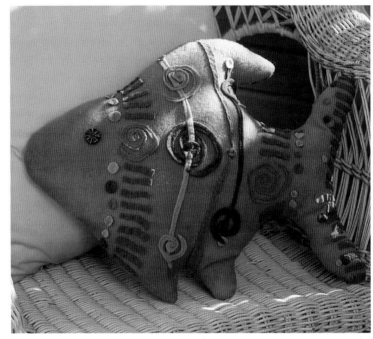

Flashy Fish Pillow on page 51

Photo 2

From top right to bottom left: fabric stabilizer, glue stick, fray preventive; craft/fabric glue, fusible interfacing, fusible webbing, and doubled-sided tape.

Straight Pins

Straight pins are used to hold fabrics and embellishments in place until they are secured by some type of adhesive or thread. It is recommend that you have a box of pins marked "glue pins". Many of the pins used to hold glued items in place retain some of the glue on the shaft. This can cause snags in finer woven fabrics but does not affect the wool when used. Keep these pins away from fine fabrics. (Photo 3)

Cutting Tools

There are various cutting tools that can be used to cut the materials used in this book. A pair of craft scissors and fabric shears are an important part of each project. Avoid using fabric shears on anything but fabric. Rotary cutters and a self-healing cutting mat are helpful in creating straight accurate cuts. Craft knives come in several sizes are helpful in cutting a variety of materials. I most frequently use the smaller pencil-sized craft knives and have sharp blades on hand to keep the work neat and well cut. (Photo 4)

Photo 3

Photo 4

From top left to bottom right: fabric shears, large rotary cutter, small fabric shears, craft knife, small rotary cutter, and craft scissors.

Embellishments

Embellishments are a way to add that something extra to an appliquéd project. Beads, decorative brads, and buttons are all a wonderful way to enhance a design. These embellishments can be glued or stitched in place. Colored wire can be twisted, curled, and shaped for that special look. Using such wonderful embellishments can only make a piece of handcrafted work all the more special. (Photo 5)

Close-up of Seaside Trio on page 76

From top left to bottom right: a string beads, metal leaf dusts, colored wires, decorative brads, assorted gauge wires, beads, brass discs, buttons, and brass spacers.

Photo 5

STITCHES TO KNOW

BUTTONHOLE STITCH

1. Bring needle up at A; go down at B. Come up again at C, keeping thread under needle. Go down at D.

2. Repeat, making all stitches equal.

FRENCH KNOT

1. Bring needle up at A. Wrap ribbon loosely two or three times around needle close to sharp point.

2. Hold ribbon off to one side as you gently insert needle next to entry hole.

3. Hold this knot until ribbon is pulled all the way through to back of fabric.

OUTLINE STITCH

1. Bring needle up at A, keeping floss to the right and above the needle. Go down at B; come up at C.

2. Repeat as necessary.

SLIP STITCH

1. Bring needle up between fold at A.

2. Go down at B and slide needle between fold for ⅛" to ¼".

3. Bring needle up through both folds at same level as A, but over a small distance as shown in diagram.

4. Draw up thread gently to secure a closed joint, too hard will pucker fabric.

5. Repeat stitch across entire opening, keeping stitches between ⅛" and ¼" apart.

STRAIGHT STITCH

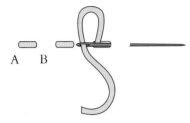

1. Bring needle up at A. Go down at B.

2. Repeat, leaving an unstitched area between each stitch.

3. Repeat, covering entire area.

WHIPSTITCH

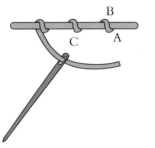

1. Bring needle up through both layers of fabric at A. Draw thread out.

2. Go down at B; come up at C in one motion, catching two or three threads.

3. Draw thread out gently. Repeat, covering entire area to secure fabric from raveling.

ZIGZAG STITCH

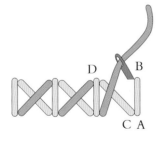

1. Bring needle up at A, using three strands of thread.

2. Go down at B; come up at C. Go down at D, diagonally. Repeat working right to left.

3. Repeat along entire length, working left to right.

TIPS

Sewing Tips:

- Using a sewing machine for your project is a great option. Wool tends to leave a great deal of lint in the machine, so clean your machine frequently.

- For freemotion sewing on a machine, lower your feed dogs and use a darning foot. There are many choices; right now I prefer to use the closed foot because it does not catch on the wool pieces. I also use a foot that allows cord and ribbon to be inserted through an opening and allows the machine to sew over the cord as you move along. I have sewn on cord without that foot, too. A little practice of freemotion sewing and sewing cord on scraps is always a good idea.

- For hand-sewing, use needles that fit the fiber being used. Large-eyed needles are often a must.

- Use a safety pin to help turn a long tube of fabric inside out.

Finishing Tips:

- If using glass to cover your project, avoid having the glass resting on the wool, use spacers that will lift the glass away from the work.

- If choosing to not use glass to cover your project, remember to remove dust from your project periodically with a sticky lint roller or a vacuum hose attachment with the end covered in a netting or piece of pantihose, holding the end of the hose away from the surface a little bit to not disturb the embellishments. Occasionally, you may need to reglue embellishments as you clean them with these two methods, but eventually you will have things securely in place.

NATURE'S CREATIONS

THREE BIRDS PANEL

This panel is quite large but was surprisingly quick to finish. Remember that any project can be altered to suit your needs, skills, and patience level. Adjust the size, the color, and the design by making changes before you begin and even during the working process.

ITEMS TO GATHER

- General Items on page 10
- Wools:
  10" sq. gray for bird
  14" x 3½" light blue for sky strip
  14" x 3½" light green for grass strip
  14" x 6½" forest green for grass strip
  14" x 8" medium blue for sky strip
  20" x 8" brown for tree branches
  20" x 25" black for background
  30" x 36" gray blue for panel backing
  scraps: light blue; gray/brown tweed; light forest
      green; medium forest green; yellow
- Beading needles
- Beads: glass; brass; precious stones
- Threads: browns; grays; assorted greens; metallics

INSTRUCTIONS

1. Enlarge 200% and photocopy Three Birds Panel Patterns on pages 108–110. *Note: If desired, pattern can be traced directly from book with tracing paper.* Cut out Large Black Bird and Small Black Bird from black wool. Cut out Gray Bird from gray wool. Cut out Branch I, Branch II, and Branch III from brown wool. Cut out leaves from green wool scraps. Cut beaks, bird accent pieces, and stars from remaining wool scraps.

2. Lay the wool pieces out on a flat surface. Refer to Pattern Placement below. Set aside the leaves, tree branches, and stars. *Notes: Now is the time to make major changes with this piece if desired. Do not work with the largest blue fabric until it is time to do the work that overlaps on to it—too much bulk to handle.*

Pattern Placement

3. Stitch the beaks, wings, and bird accent pieces onto the birds. The largest bird on the left has its tail cut off in this pattern; work on the two pieces separately. *Note: You will have an easier time working the decorative stitches with the birds in your hand and will only have to secure the birds in place with a straight stitch around the edges when you are ready.*

4. Lay the medium blue, light blue, light green, and forest green wool pieces onto the black background, overlapping each piece approximately ½". Pin each layer in order (or glue sparingly). Straight-stitch the background edges.

5. Randomly long straight-stitch the green pieces with variegated green threads, moving from the bottom of the piece to the top, sometimes crossing onto the black and the blue areas.

6. Sew the branches across the panel, adding the detached branch in place. Sew birds and some leaves onto background fabric, allowing the small black bird to cover part of the leaves. Secure in place with pins or small amounts of fabric glue.

7. Using a variety of threads and beads, stitch the pieces down. Stitch through all the layers into the black background wool. Choose stitches and fibers that add character, texture, and interest to each piece. (Photo 1)

8. Add the remaining leaves and stitch them down, leaving a few leaves unattached on one edge. Simply stitch in the same manner, but only going through the single layer of the leaf. Add the gray/blue wool piece for backing. Remove pins. *Note: This will allow you to sew on the leaves that extend beyond the black wool on to this piece.*

9. Make certain to sew through all the layers of wool including the gray/blue back piece when it is attached. Using metallic threads, stitch streaks through the sky with curves and spirals, and stitch spider webs. (Photo 2) Sew threads across and onto the edges of the wool to tie all the layers together.

10. Frame as desired.

Photo 1

Photo 2

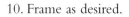

Helpful Suggestions

The panel can now be finished by adding a hanging sleeve to the top of the piece on the back, or have the piece framed using acid-free materials. If adding glass to framed work, make certain the glass does not touch the wool. Use a spacer to lift the glass up from the wool itself.

Variations

Vary the colors of the birds, the lay out of the design, or the background colors. Add more objects to the fabric. Hang the panel from an actual tree branch. The Variation Drawings below show some variations pulled from the panel. The wide panel that is attached to the branch has a variety of birds on it, a good opportunity to work with color and shapes. The tabs on the panel can vary in length to accommodate the branch's shape. Vary the shape of the panel to mirror the wonderful curves in a branch. The narrow horizontal drawing of chubby chicks can be really fun, using a rainbow of colors. Or create a black-and-white checkered look behind the birds. What other colors could go behind the birds—you are in charge—choose. How about a nest to go with your birds? Use the wonderful fibers available, add a few twigs, bits of wire, then find a wonderful piece of wool for the eggs. Use chalks, markers, and gold-leaf flakes to color the eggs.

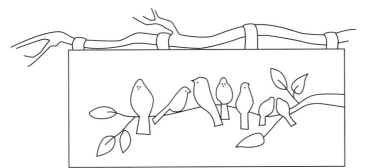

Variation Drawings

BIRDS WITH ATTITUDE

ITEMS TO GATHER

- General Items on page 10
- Wools for Black Bird:
  6" x 8" black for bottom wing
  6" x 8" black/white plaid for top wing
  11" x 9" red/black houndstooth for body
- Wools for Bluebird of Humbleness:
  6" x 8" purple for bottom wing
  6" x 8" red for top wing
  11" x 9" blue for body
  Scraps for feathers
- Wools for Yellow Pudgie Bird:
  ½" x 10" crimson for fringe
  ½" x 10" yellow for bottom wing accent
  6'" x 8" purple for top wing
  6" x 8" yellow for bottom wing
  11" x 9" orange for body
- 6" wooden candleholder for base (3)
- 20-gauge wire (5")
- Acrylic paints
- Beads for Black Bird:
  assorted for wings
  black bugle for wings and tail
  black flat beads for eyes (2)
  black wooden for wings and tail
  red glass for eyes (2) *Note: Make certain the black flat beads are larger than the red glass beads since the beads will be stacked for the eyes.*
- Beads for Bluebird of Humbleness: glass; brass spacer
- Brads: ½"-square decorative; assorted colored brads for Yellow Pudgie Bird
- Colorful variegated fiber for Bluebird of Humbleness (3 yds)
- Paintbrush
- Pointed tool for defining turned-out corners
- Polyester stuffing
- Semigloss paint sealer
- Tweezers

BLACK BIRD

Instructions for Black Bird

1. Paint candleholder, or base, to match bird. Allow to dry. *Note: You may wish to just do the main color and finish the detail work when you see the finished bird.*

2. Enlarge 200% and photocopy Birds with Attitude Patterns on page 111. Cut two body pieces and a tail piece from black wool. *Notes: If using a fabric that has a right and wrong side, reverse the pattern so that you will not have two sides facing the same direction. The attitude of the bird can be greatly influenced at this stage simply by moving the opening along the belly of the bird.*

3. Sew the two sides together, using a ¼" seam allowance. Make certain to not sew up the opening.

4. Gently turn the bird body right side out. Use a pointed tool to encourage the beak, tail, and other areas of the profile to fully extend.

5. Make certain the top of the base will fit into the opening; if it does not, loosen the threads at the opening to allow it to fit.

6. Stuff the body of the bird firmly; use the tool you turned the wool with to help you reach all the areas of the body. Check frequently to ensure a proper fit of the base. *Note: What you want is for the base to fit far enough into the body to be a support and also to be able to see the features of the base that you like.* When satisfied with the look of the body and fit at the base, remove the base and apply glue around the top of the base and carefully reinsert it into the bird. Tuck the ends of the opening up to the inside around the base and glue or sew in place. Check the position of the bird and the base to make certain it is the way you want it. Set aside to dry.

7. Cut the bottom wing from black wool. Cut the top wing from black/white plaid. Layer the wing pieces together with the smaller piece on top. Align the wings at the top and make certain that there is an even amount of the bottom wing showing. Pin the tail in place under both wings. Stitch a wide zigzag down the center of the wings and tail through all the layers with either a contrasting color or one that blends well with the fabric.

8. Stitch assorted beads along the top wing and black wooden beads with an occasional contrasting bead along the edge of the black wing. Stitch black bugle beads in a chevron pattern down the center of the tail and across the top wing. (Photo 1)

9. Insert wire or a straightened large paper clip under the zigzag stitching on the underside of the wing to give shape to the wings.

10. Use fabric glue to attach the wings to the back of the bird. Hold in place for a few seconds. *Notes: You may want to stitch the wings in place at the top and the bottom for added security. Be aware that you have the ability to place the wings forward towards the head, centered, or more towards the tail. You may glue both wings together or leave the top wing unattached except where it has been sewn at the center.*

Photo 1

11. Stitch the eyes on by pulling the threaded needle from one side of the head to the other, leaving the knot on one side and through a large bead, into a smaller bead, back through the large bead, then out through to the original side. Pick up a large bead and pull the thread through, thread on the smaller bead, then pass the thread once again through the large bead. Guide the needle and thread back into the opposite side. Knot and secure underneath the large bead. Trim the thread.

12. Finish painting the base as desired.

13. Seal with a semigloss finish.

YELLOW PUDGIE BIRD

Instructions for Yellow Pudgie Bird

1. Make the Yellow Pudgie Bird, following instructions for the Black Bird, Steps 1–13 on pages 22–24 with the following variations:

   ▪ Before stuffing the body of the bird, apply the brads to the breast area.

   ▪ The wings are made with a little more detail. The top wing is edged with a crimson fringe made from the ½" x 10" piece of wool. Before applying the fringe to the wing, clip along the wing edge to within ⅛" of the opposite edge. Glue fringe to the underside of the purple wing along the outside edge, showing about ⅜". Hold in place for a few seconds. Apply colorful brads all over the top wing. For the bottom wing accent, cut the yellow strip of wool in half. Glue to either side of blue wing.

Allow about ⅛" of the yellow edging to show.

▪ For the tail, more crimson wool was fringed and applied down the tail. (Photo 2)

▪ Before applying the wings to the back of the bird, add a ½"-square decorative brad to the top of the wing to act as an accent and stitch beads between the halves.

▪ Attach the glass bead and brass spacer in the same manner as for the eyes on the Black Bird, Step 11 on page 24. (Photo 3)

Photo 2

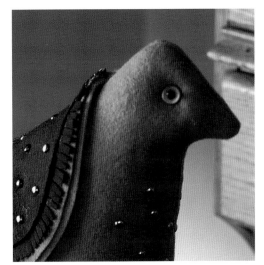

Photo 3

Cut the under wing and tail for a more ragged look.

Freehand-cut the decorative feathers from wool scraps. Glue a piece of variegated fiber along the spine. Glue the feathers to the top wing at one end, allowing the feathers to float up. (Photo 5)

Glue the fibers, wire, and beads to the base with a strong glue, to carry out the humble theme of the bird.

No sealer was applied to the base so that a very flat finish would match the wool look.

Photo 5

BLUEBIRD OF HUMBLENESS

Instructions for Bluebird of Humbleness

1. Make the Bluebird of Humbleness following instructions for the Black Bird, Steps 1–12 on pages 22–24 with the following variations:

   Rotate bird forward a little, to a more horizontal position. (Photo 4)

HELPFUL SUGGESTIONS

Before cutting out the bird's body, determine its attitude by where you place the opening, mark this on the pattern, then cut out the body. Use tweezers to place the beads when gluing and to guide the fiber where you want it to go. Remember these are your projects; you have control over how they turn out.

VARIATIONS

Vary the fabric used on the birds. Try cotton, silk, or oilcloth. Use a different type of base such as glass, an old funnel or oil can, an antique bobbin or thread spool, or a piece of pine with the bark. Embellish with beads, ribbons, wires, metal accent pieces, or mirrors.

Photo 4

BIRD PURSE

ITEMS TO GATHER

- General Items on page 10
- Wools:
  4" x 7" bright blue for bird body
  4" x 7" light orange for bird body
  10" sq. burnt orange for purse front
  10" sq. light burnt orange for purse back
  assorted scraps: brown; gold; green; pink for design
    on purse front
- 18" x 24" coordinating cotton fabric for lining,
  pocket and binding

- Accenting colored cords: 28" length for purse strap (2);
  2½" length for loop around large bead
- Assorted threads
- Clear plastic flowers (5)
- Pointed tool
- Red beads: ½" disks (4); ⅝" large; medium (10);
  small (5)

Instructions for Purse Front

1. Enlarge 200% and photocopy Bird Purse Patterns on page 112. Cut purse pattern from burnt orange pieces for the purse front and back.

2. Fold cotton fabric right sides together. Using the purse pattern, cut two pieces at once for the lining. Cut ½" x 24" strip from the same fabric for the binding. *Note: This length may need to be pieced.*

3. Cut the bird's body from the light orange wool. Cut a second bird's body ⅛" larger all around from bright blue wool.

4. Cut the leaves and branches from wool scraps. Cut the wing from light orange wool. Cut the wing accent from gold wool scrap. Lay out the pattern pieces on the purse back to desired look. *Note: This will allow you to make adjustments to the design until it pleases you; and by having the back side by side with the front, you can keep the design intact while re-creating it on the front piece.*

5. Transfer the branch pieces and the leaves to the purse front. Pin the pieces on or sparingly apply fabric glue to the pieces to hold them in place. *Note: If gluing, carefully secure the pieces to the wool. Add more glue if necessary.* Allow to dry, then begin to sew. Sew two of the leaves along the center line only. Remove pins. Apply a fray preventative to these edges if the wool is of a loose weave.

6. Cut a strip ½" wide by the length of the wing from the shoulder to tip of wing from pink wool scrap. Clip the strip on one side ¼" in to the fabric, spacing about ¼" wide, creating fringe.

7. Add the pink fringe ⅛"–¼" under the curved edge of the wing. Pin or lightly glue in place. Apply the gold wing accent piece with glue or a whipstitch. Refer to Whipstitch on page 15. (Photo 1) Attach the wing to the body of the bird with a little glue or pins.

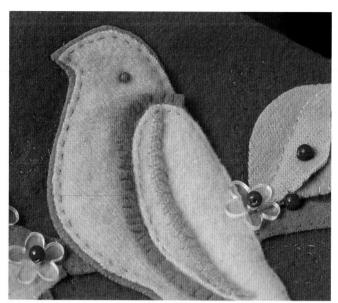

Photo 1

8. Topstitch around the body of the bird on the orange wool about ⅛" in from the edge, leaving the blue layer free (unstitched). Topstitch along the pink edge of the wing, then pull the stitches a little to give some dimension to the stitching.

9. Stitch one small red bead onto the bird for an eye. (Photo 2)

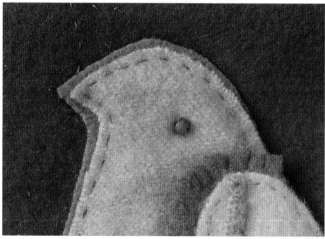

Photo 2

10. Add some straight-stitch lines and curves to purse front between the appliquéd pieces with a heavier thread that has a subtle but a contrasting color. Refer to Straight Stitch on page 15. (Photo 3)

Photo 3

11. Secure flowers onto purse front by stitching a large bead into the center hole of the flower. (Photo 4) *Note: The bead holds the clear flower in place when it is stitched on through the hole in the flower.* Stitch on additional red beads as accent pieces.

Photo 4

INSTRUCTIONS FOR PURSE LINING

1. Cut 4" x 6" piece from cotton lining fabric for the pocket.

2. Fold this piece in half lengthwise (4" x 3"), right sides together, and press. Sew around the edge, using ¼" seam allowance and leaving an opening large enough to turn the fabric through. Trim the corners of the square close to the seam line. Turn the lining right side out. Make certain the corners are fully extended. If necessary, use a pointed tool. Press the pocket and tuck the opening edges into the inside. Position the pocket to one side of the lining and center. Topstitch in place, sewing down one side, across the bottom and up the other side. *Note: You can use an iron-on adhesive tape to make the pocket by pressing the pocket with the right sides facing out, folding the cut edges into the center of the piece and inserting the adhesive between the pieces, positioned just inside the fabric. Iron as instructed. Use the adhesive strips to attach the pocket onto the lining.*

3. Place the lining with the pocket and the unadorned backing piece of wool together, right side of lining facing in. Pin across the top. Fold a 2½" length of cord in half for loop closure. Center and pin loop closure ends on top edge of lining between the lining and the wool. Use the large red bead to help judge the size of the loop needed. *Note: Gauge the size of the loop by the size of the large bead. Measure the bead to ensure a good fit around it when closing.* Sew the pieces, right sides together. Using a ½" seam allowance, sew along the top of the fabric where pinned. Repeat with purse front and remaining lining piece.

4. Press the pieces at the seam to set the stitches, then turn the front and the back pieces right sides out. Line the edges of purse front and back up as evenly as possible. Make certain the top is even and the lining is not showing over the top of the front or back wool pieces. Trim around the combined sides and make certain they are even with each other.

5. Find the top center of the purse front. Using a heavy thread, stitch on the large bead. Stitch from the inside at seam between the front and back fabrics, pulling the threads through at this point so as not to show any stitches on the front or back of the piece. Stitch the thread through the bead several times. (Photo 5)

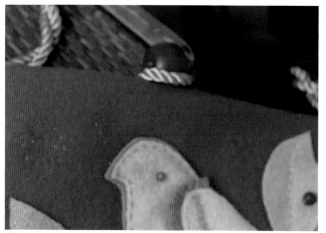

Photo 5

6. Attach the long pieces of cord to each corner of the purse front, positioning them at a slight angle inward so that when the purse is sewn together the cord ends will only be sewn.

7. Sew the front and back of the purse together, right sides facing out. Line the two top corners carefully to ensure a good match. Sew along the outside edges, using a ¼" seam allowance.

8. To apply the binding, cut a strip 1½" wide by the length of the perimeter of the purse (not including the opening). Fold to the inside ½" of the fabric at one end to make a fold at the top. Line up the folded edge with the top of the purse at one corner, making certain that the right side of the binding fabric is facing the right side of the purse. Pin the edge of the binding to the purse, starting at the top corner. Have the rest of the binding extend into the center of the purse. After pinning around the purse to the other

corner, trim the excess binding away, remembering to allow ½" of the binding to be folded in at this end as with the start. Carefully pin the binding to the corner.

9. Sew the binding to the purse, using a ½" seam allowance. Turn the binding around to the back of the purse. Fold under the binding edge into the center of the binding to the point that the fold you are making aligns with the stitching from the front. Pin into place and hand-stitch the binding into the back of the purse. Slip-stitch the ends of the binding closed at each end. Refer to Slip Stitch on page 14. (Photo 6)

Photo 6

10. Stitch the disks and small beads to either side of the purse at the point where the cord is attached. (Photo 7)

Photo 7

Helpful Suggestions

This project can be easily done with glue, using iron-on adhesive tape and a good fabric glue. The lining for the purse can be attached to the wool with fusible interfacing. You can turn the top of each piece into the center to cover the raw edges of the lining fabric before ironing the pieces together. The wool in this case does not fray because it was washed and dried—"felted." The cotton, however, is very good at fraying so you may consider other means to cover up the raw edges.

To secure the two purse sides together, you can use strong fabric glue or a tape product that when ironed can securely hold where it is placed. Place the lining sides together and go for it. To attach the purse straps, a large grommet can be inserted at each corner of the purse, the cords can then be passed through the holes and knotted to secure the ends. A dab of glue can be placed on the cut ends of the cord to keep them from fraying.

To cover the edges of the purse, a piece of felted wool can be cut wide enough to overlap the edges well, and long enough to come up to the corners of the bag. The edging can be cut with decorative-edged scissors to add interest.

Back view of Bird Purse

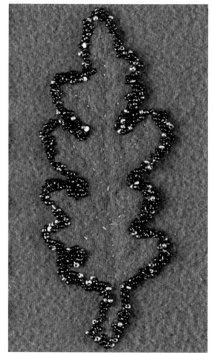
FOUR-LEAF PANEL

This design lends itself well to hand- and machine-stitching as well as gluing. When gluing, be careful of the amount of adhesive used so that the excess does not detract from the project. There are double-sided adhesive sheets that are very strong and would hold the wool pieces well in this situation. Both non-iron-on and heat-activated adhesives may be used. To attach the beads use a strong fabric or craft glue.

ITEMS TO GATHER

■ General Items on page 10
■ Wools:
  ½" sq. light green for stacked squares (54)
  ⅝" sq. dark gold for stacked squares (54)
  assorted scraps: dark gold; light gold; dark green; light sage; plaid *Note: The ginkgo leaf has been reverse appliquéd to the wool for that reason the leaf wool needs to be larger than its pattern piece.*
■ Beading needle
■ Beads: glass in a variety of sizes and colors (55); old brass spacers (16)
■ Cord
■ Threads: copper; light gold twill; metallic; dark green; variegated light green

INSTRUCTIONS

1. Photocopy Leaf #1, #2, #3, and Ginkgo Leaf Patterns on page 113. Cut Leaf #1 from dark gold scrap. Cut Leaf #2 from dark green plaid scrap. Cut Leaf #3 from light gold scrap.

2. Lay the three cut out leaves and ginkgo leaf pattern in desired order on the sage green wool. Trace around ginkgo leaf with washable fabric marker. Trim along this line and remove the inside piece. Cut a piece from light green wool large enough to cover entire opening of the piece. Pin in place from the back side of the opening.

3. Glue, stitch, or pin all of the leaves in place. Embellish as desired.

4. Straight-stitch veining onto the dark gold leaf with metallic thread. Outline the dark gold leaf with a variety of glass beads. Refer to Straight Stitch on page 15. *Note: A machine-stitch could be used here instead of the beading.* (Photo 1)

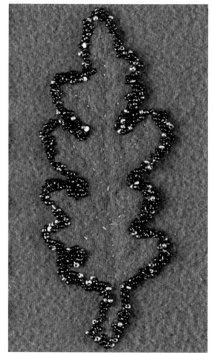

Photo 1

5. Using a reverse buttonhole stitch, sew around the ginkgo leaf edges with metallic thread. Randomly add French knots to the veining with variegated light green thread. Refer to Buttonhole Stitch and French Knot on page 14. (Photo 2)

6. Buttonhole-stitch around edges of dark green plaid leaf with a dark green thread. Stitch old brass spacers at corners where the plaids cross. (Photo 3)

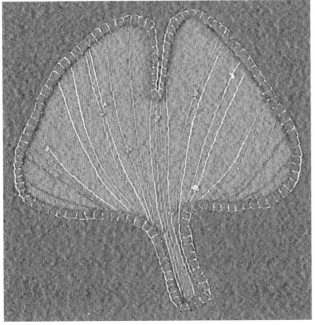

Photo 2

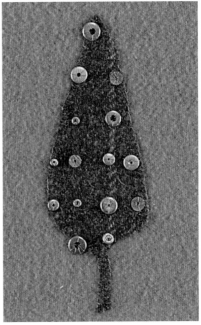

Photo 3

7. Whipstitch cord approximately ⅛" inside the edge of light gold leaf. Stitch a bead where one end of the cord meets the other end. Refer to Whipstitch on page 15. (Photo 4)

8. Center and place one light sage felt square onto one dark gold wool square.

9. Sew glass bead to center of layered squares with a copper thread. Buttonhole-stitch the bottom square with a light gold twill thread to the background fabric. Stitch the top square with a copper thread. Repeat 53 times for border. (Photo 5)

Helpful Suggestions

If hand-sewing, each square can be sewn together before attaching or sewing one layer at a time in place. Gluing would be quick and easy, and a decorative leaf can be machine-sewn instead of the squares.

Variations

The finished leaf panel can be used as a table runner, wall hanging, or framed for a wall. By changing the colors and textures of the fabrics used, you can achieve a quite different look. Instead of the wool squares being used to frame the leaves, you can find or make copper leaves and use them in a border. Small squares of cork or wood, acorn tops, twigs, etc., would add a nice touch to the variations for this project.

Photo 4

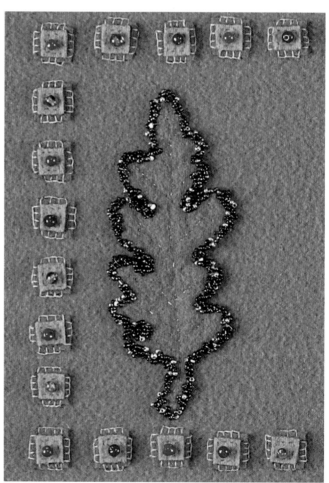

Photo 5

GINKGO LEAF TABLE RUNNER

ITEMS TO GATHER

- General Items on page 10
- Wools:
  18" x 36" beige/oatmeal
  assorted scraps: shades of green for 21 leaves
- 27" x 48" coordinating cotton fabric for border
- Assorted beads
- Colorful cord
- Threads: assorted; green twill; light green variegated for free-motion machine-sewing

INSTRUCTIONS

1. Photocopy the Ginkgo Leaf Patterns on page 113. *Note: If desired, pattern can be traced directly from book with tracing paper.* Cut 21 leaves from green scraps in a variety of sizes.

2. Lightly glue all the leaves in place on the beige wool. *Note: If you choose to have several of the leaves overlapping onto the border fabric, apply them later.*

3. Sew the veining onto each leaf with green twill thread. (Photo 1) *Note: If doing this on your sewing machine, drop the feed dogs and use a darning or open toe foot. This will allow you to move freely about the leaf. If you haven't done free-form quilting, practice on a piece of paper with a pencil or use sewing machine and an unthreaded needle to practice on a sheet of paper until you are comfortable to move to a practice piece of fabric.*

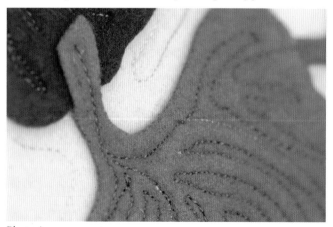

Photo 1

4. Change the top thread to a spool of light green variegated thread and begin to free-motion-sew onto the background fabric. Use any pattern of stitching desired. (Photo 2) *Note: You can draw out your pattern with a washable fabric marker and trace around that if you want. Or use hand-sewing on the leaves and background instead of the machine-sewing.*

Photo 2

5. When you have completed the sewing, remeasure the wool piece and trim if necessary to obtain straight edges and even measurements. Lay the wool onto the center of the cotton fabric. *Note: The right side of the cotton is facing down and the decorated side of the wool is facing up and centered on the cotton fabric.* Fold the edges of the backing over the wool covering only ½" of the wool. Fold ¼" under at this point to make a smooth overlapping border. Iron the remaining fabric flat, forming a frame around the piece. Pin in place. *Note: You can adjust the width of the border by trimming it down where it overlaps the wool.*

6. When the edges are all an even width and the overlapping fold is at least ¼" under and still covering the wool edges, pin in place and press flat.

7. To secure the border to the center and apply the decorative cord, use one of the following methods: (Photo 3)

   a. Using cording foot, machine-sew around the border, sewing down the cord and the edge down simultaneously.

   b. If hand-sewing or if a more casual look is desired, slip-stitch the cord to the backing fabric. Refer to Slip Stitch on page 14.

Photo 3

8. Apply the leaves that overlap onto the border, using the same method as in Step 2 on page 36. (Photo 4)

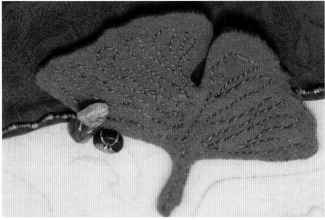

Photo 4

9. Stitch several accent beads onto the seam of the border. (Photo 5)

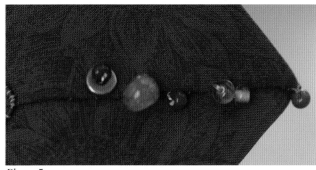

Photo 5

10. Stitch several accent beads onto the table runner for dimension and sparkle. (Photo 6)

Photo 6

Helpful Suggestions

For an all-glued project, fusible interfacing can be used to attach the backing. The folded border can be placed on with iron-on fusible tape. The leaves can be glued on with fabric glue and the veining can be done by carefully gluing on decorative threads or fibers. The background details can be added with fabric paint or chalks.

Single Tree Panel

A portrait of an umbrella tree is framed here to remind me of that special time when the day is beginning to close. The sun is glinting off the edges of the canopy of leaves and a few early stars are peeking out of the pale sky, and the horizon is showing a little color from the fading sunset. I don't know if any of this is possible at one time but I liked the way it looked in wool.

Items to Gather

- General Items on page 10
- Wools:
  ½" x 5¼" strips: dark coral; light coral; light pink for sunset
  4" x 8" dark green for treetop
  7" x 12" light blue for sky
  13" x 16" brown tweed
  light moss green scraps for fringe
- Beading needle
- Beads: seed beads; small bugle beads; white pearlized
- Brown mohair
- Frame (optional)
- Threads: brown; light-colored sheen; dark coral; light coral; dark green; light pink

Instructions

1. Enlarge 200% and photocopy Single Tree Pattern on page 114.

2. Lay the tree trunk pattern onto the light blue wool, aligning the bottoms of the trunk pattern and the fabric. Trace around the pattern and carefully cut out the trunk from the blue wool. Set the trunk and the five small sky pieces that are around the branches aside.

3. Lay the blue wool onto the brown tweed background, about 2" down from the top, comparing the positions with the pattern. Tack the sky pieces into place with fabric glue stick. (Photo 1)

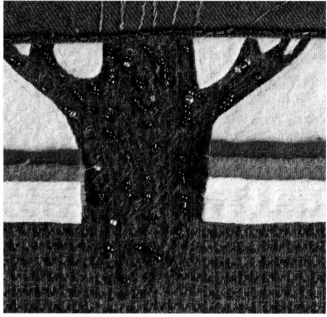

Photo 1

4. Cut the treetop from the dark green wool and place just at the top of the tree limbs, tack in place.

5. Overlap the ½" strips: the dark coral is first, the light coral, then the pink. Place them on either side of the tree trunk.

Photo 2

6. Using a needle and long straight stitches, attach the strips to the background with matching thread. *Note: The stitches vary in length on each strip with the pink strip having three layers of stitching.* Refer to Straight Stitch on page 15. (Photo 2)

7. Lay the brown mohair fibers in vertical "stripes," simulating the natural ridging in a tree trunk. Using brown thread, stitch the mohair to the tweed background. Periodically add a seed bead or larger bead to accent the trunk. Carry the fibers up onto the limbs of the tree. (Photo 3)

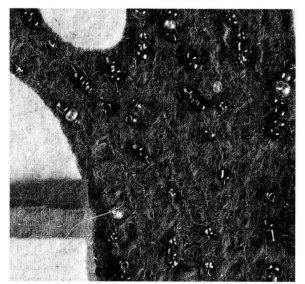

Photo 3

8. Using a light-colored thread, stitch some horizontal lines from the dark coral strip up into the sky area. Gradually widen the space between the lines as you move upward. Continue stitching on each side of the trunk, making certain to align the horizontal lines evenly across from each other.

9. Stitch a few pearlized seed beads across the sky.

10. Stitch small bugle beads across the bottom of the treetop, making certain the beads line up against each other closely. (Photo 4)

Photo 4

11. Stitch branches coming up from the tree limbs with dark green thread, but not in the sky areas.

12. Cut several ½"-wide strips from light moss green wool to desired length. Snip away at the lengths and have the pieces ready to attach to the treetop. *Note: You could also measure around the curve of the tree and use that to determine to the lengths of the ½"-wide strips.*

13. Straight–stitch along the treetop edge to catch each strip one at a time and attach them around the perimeter of the treetop. (Photo 5)

14. Frame as desired.

Variations

You can easily vary this design by adding more trees in a row, or in groups as in a field. Change the size and color of your fabrics. Add more beads and layers of fringe.

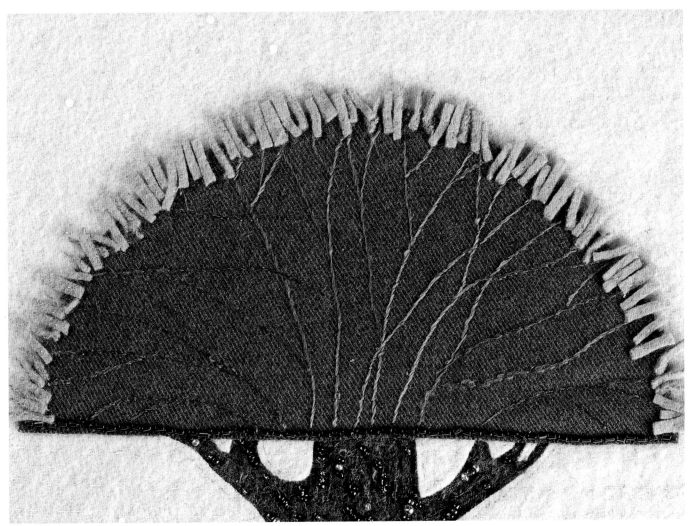

Photo 5

FOUR SEASONS WALL HANGING

This is a simple pattern which is shown here as a *rough-cut, primitive look. There is only on kind of stitch used—a straight stitch. Sometimes it crosses itself, other times it just stabs away and mostly the straight stitch just follows straight lines. This project can go from just using glue to elaborate sewing by machine or by hand. The fabric glue can successfully attach fibers to outline and accent as well as any other methods of embellishment. It is up to you to choose, single out or combine what you like.*

ITEMS TO GATHER

- General Items on page 10
- Wools:
  4" sq. assorted blues (4)
  12" x 18" beige wool
  14" x 22" navy
  scraps: brown prints or solids; light gold; light gray; medium gray; light orange; dark pink; light pink
- ⅛"-wide green silk ribbon
- ⅛" dia. 24" wooden dowel or thin branch

INSTRUCTIONS

1. Choose four blue shades from the wool for the four seasons squares: cool spring, winter colors, warm summer, and fall colors. *Note: The background, tree trunk, and leaf canopy need to combine to also appear as spring, summer, autumn, and winter colors.*

2. Enlarge 200% and photocopy Four Season's Wall Hanging Pattern on page 114. Cut four treetops and four trunks from wool scraps.

3. Cut four ¼" x 4" strips from wool scraps for the horizon line.

4. Using fabric glue, attach each piece onto the blue square in order: treetop first, the horizon line second, then lay the trunk overlapping the bottom edges of the first two. If hand-sewing, glue sparingly where you will be sewing. (Photo 1) *Note: Some fraying may occur, if that bothers you or there is too much fraying use the iron-on facing on the back of each piece. Prepare the approximate size needed, iron-on according to the manufacturer's instructions. Cut out each piece after it is ironed from the combined wool and interfacing, making certain the back of the facing does not show beyond the edges.*

Photo 1

5. Position each blue square onto the beige fabric and glue into place.

6. Finish adding decorative elements, using one of the following method:

   a. For an all-glue project, proceed with gluing carefully. Add decorative cord, more wool accents, beads, etc.

   b. For hand-sewing or machine-sewing, first stitch around the perimeter of each square with a neutral color thread. *Note: The thread will appear slightly different on each square.* (Photo 2) Using an accent or contrasting color, add stitching to embellish each tree. (Photo 3)

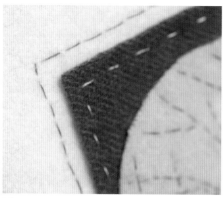

Photo 2

Photo 3

7. Cut ribbon into two 13" lengths and one 12" length. Knot each ribbon end and straight-stitch in place. Refer to Straight Stitch on page 115. (Photo 4)

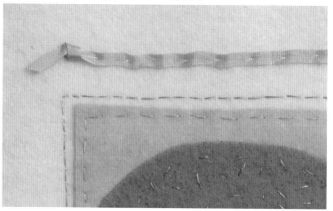

Photo 4

8. Position beige rectangle on navy wool backing with more blue wool showing at the bottom than at the top, leaving approximately 1" of fabric showing on the top and the sides. Pin or glue in place. *Note: If you are using a woven fabric for backing instead of the wool, you can fray the edges.* (Photo 5)

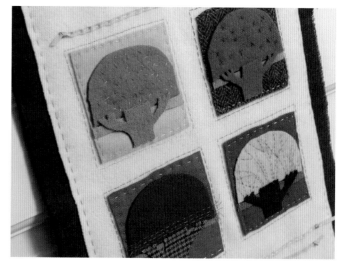

Photo 5

9. Stitch perimeter of the beige wool rectangle. (Photo 6)

Photo 6

10. Run two stitching lines parallel to each other about 1" down from the top of the beige rectangle and 1" apart, creating a channel for the wooden dowel. (Photo 7) *Note: If you are using a branch, adjust the size of the channel to fit or lay the branch across the top of the beige rectangle and sew around the branch with decorative thread, catching the wool backing in the process.*

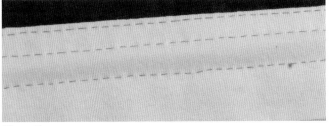

Photo 7

11. Insert the dowel into channel.

12. Tie one end of cord to each end of the dowel, creating a hanger. (Photo 8)

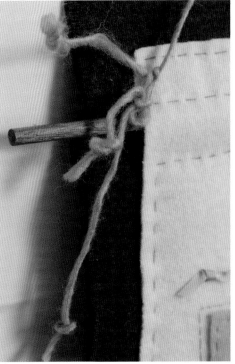

Photo 8

Close-up of each tree

THERE IS ONE IN EVERY CROWD

There is one in every crowd especially in this fish picture. The number of rows, the size of the fish, and number of fish used for this project will be determined by the size of your background fabric. Feel free to embellish some or all of the fish with beads, ribbons, scraps of wool, etc. You can also use a variety of fish sizes.

ITEMS TO GATHER

- General Items on page 10
- Wools:
  assorted colored scraps for fish and embellishments
  hand-dyed watercolor patterned for background
- Assorted embellishments: beads, ribbons, etc.
- Assorted embroidery floss
- Frame (optional)

INSTRUCTIONS

1. Enlarge or reduce and photocopy Fish Pattern on page 115 as desired for desired number of fish. *Note: If desired, pattern can be traced directly from book with tracing paper.*

2. Cut out fish from desired wool scraps. *Note: If using patterned material for fish, remember to determine which way the pattern will face before cutting the wool. Determine the spacing of the fish pattern(s).*

3. Layout the fish in rows, patterns, and colors as desired. *Note: You will be removing these fish in order to embellish them, so to make it easier to return to their proper place, I suggest making a pattern or numbering them on paper.* (Photo 1)

Photo 1

4. Hand-sew, machine-sew, and/or glue embellishments onto fish. If hand-sewing the embellishments, make certain to periodically catch the backing fabric not just the fish fabric when adding embellishments. This will help secure the fish and give it a more dimensional effect. (Photo 2)

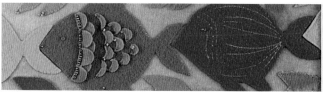
Photo 2

5. Attach fish to background fabric by hand-sewing or gluing. For stability when hand-sewing, catch the backing fabric frequently. *Note: I used a lot of chain stitching with one or two strands of thick thread because it seemed more organic. I also did not necessarily space my stitching evenly, giving it more of a free-spirited outcome.*

6. Frame as desired.

FISH MOBILE

When thinking about a mobile, the first thing that may come to mind is a mobile in a baby's room. That would be a great place for the following project to end up; but think about the areas of your kitchen, child's room, family room, or wherever the space would be enlivened by some fishy friends. Keep this in mind when deciding on your color scheme.

ITEMS TO GATHER

- General Items on page 10
- Wools:
  assorted scraps: enough for two fish to be cut from each color
- ⅛" dia. 14" wooden dowels (2)
- 20-gauge wire
- Acrylic paint to match fish fabric
- Assorted embellishments: buttons; ribbon
- Beads: pot-shaped wooden beads (5); round
- Clips
- Fish line
- Flat-nosed wire cutters
- Paintbrush
- Stuffing material for fish
- Transparent tape

INSTRUCTIONS

1. Paint dowels with acrylic paint. Allow to dry.

2. Photocopy Fish Pattern on page 115. *Note: If desired, pattern can be traced directly from book with tracing paper.*

3. Cut out desired number of fish pairs from wool. *Note: If using a patterned material, make certain to reverse one fish pattern so that the right sides face correctly.*

4. Place first half from one pair right side down on work surface. Apply glue around edges of fish, then place stuffing material in center.

5. Place second half of pair over first half, right side up, matching the edges. Hold or clip in place until dry.

6. Repeat Steps 4–5 for each fish pair until desired number of is achieved.

7. Evenly trim the edges of each fish so that all edges match.

8. Cut two 2"–3" pieces from wire for fish hooks.

Photo 1

9. Curl one end of wire into a flat coil. Insert straight end through the tip of fish's nose, then make a "U" shape with the wire and bend end down at a 45° angle to resemble the end of a fish hook. Flatten hook out and trim as desired. *Note: If wire does not pierce fabric, use a large needle to pierce a hole.* (Photo 1)

Photo 2

10. Repeat Step 9 for remaining fish hooks. (Photo 2)

11. Tie various lengths of fishing line to coiled end of each fish hook, then to wooden dowel. Make certain to have enough space between each fish so that they do not crowd each other.

12. Find and mark the center point of each dowel. Cut two 7" lengths from wire.

13. Form a small coil shape at one end of wire. Thread on a round bead, a pot-shaped bead, and another round bead, then wind the remaining length of wire around the center of one dowel once. Wrap wire back down around last bead nearest the dowel to form a decorative accent. (Photo 3)

Photo 3

14. With remaining wire length, slip one end through the newly made loop and around the dowel, forming a small loop to connect the two wires. Place three round beads on remaining end. Wrap the extending wire around the second dowel two times, ending with the wire facing up and in alignment with the other beads. Add a final bead and form a flat coil to stabilize the bead and to create a point for hanging a fish line. (Photo 4)

Photo 4

15. At each dowel end, glue a pot-shaped bead and a round bead. (Photo 5)

Photo 5

16. Tie the fish to the four dowel ends, to the center bead coil, and at points between the ends of the dowels, allowing each fish to hang at a length that allows it to move freely and provides a pleasing variety of levels. Make certain the fish are balanced. *Note: Try taping the fish line with attached fish in place first to test the fish line lengths and balance.*

FLASHY FISH PILLOW

FLASHY FISH PILLOW

How about an easy project that has a big bite to it. Imagine this fish in shiny fabric contrasting the muted wool tones. Use streamers for the fins and tail. If the fish mingles with little ones, secure all embellishments, or not use them at all.

ITEMS TO GATHER

- General Items on page 10
- Wool:
  orange (enough for desired size of fish)
- Assorted fabric scraps
- Coordinating striped cotton fabric
- Polyester stuffing
- Round "tire" shaped bead

INSTRUCTIONS

1. Enlarge 400% and photocopy Flashy Fish Pillow Pattern on page 115. Cut pattern from orange wool for fish front and striped fabric for fish back.

2. Cut out variety of dots, stripes, spirals, and small rectangles from fabric scraps. Lay out as desired on orange fish front. (Photo 1) Remember to embellish tail. (Photo 2) *Note: Feel free to mark the placement of your design with a marking pencil.*

3. Glue down each piece. Apply pressure to ensure contact and security. *Note: You may also use hand- or machine sewing to attach the pieces.*

4. Glue on bead for eye. (Photo 3) Place fish front and fish back with right sides facing. Sew the fish together, leaving an opening large enough to turn fish right side out. *Note: You may also want to stitch the bead in place.*

5. Turn the fish right side out. Stuff fish with polyester stuffing to desired fullness. Avoid a lumpy appearance. Slip-stitch opening closed. Refer to Slip Stitch on page 14.

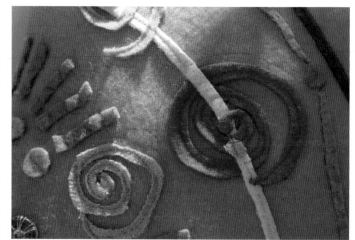
Photo 1

Photo 2

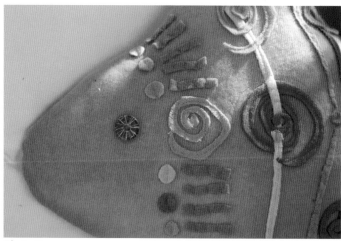
Photo 3

SIMPLY SHAPES

QUILT BLOCK TOTE

This is a tote for those who are willing to do a little sewing. It is quite simple and has a lot of potential with fabric variations and color choices. The tote has a wool front with a quilt and tin detail, and brushed flannel back, sides, and bottom. It is lined with a floral fabric with the inside front and back panels having convenient pockets added. There is also a loop for a clip on the inside to hold your keys.

ITEMS TO GATHER

- General Items on page 10
- Wools:
  4" sq. rose
  4" x 12" dark cranberry
  10" sq. rust
  16" sq. oatmeal
- 1" x ⅝" rectangular rings (2)
- 16" x 8" plastic needlework canvas
- Cotton lining fabrics: floral print (1 yd); window-pane pattern (1 yd)
- Iron-on heavy-weight fusible webbing
- Pierced tin squares: ¾" (8); 1" (2); 1½" (4)
- Turning tool or safety pin

INSTRUCTIONS FOR QUILT BLOCK

1. Cut four 1" squares, four 2" squares, and two 2¾" squares from rust color wool. Cut 2¾" squares in half on diagonal.

2. Cut two 1¼" squares and two 2" squares from dark cranberry wool. Cut each in half on diagonal. Cut four 1" squares from dark cranberry wool.

3. Cut four 1" squares from rose wool. Cut in half on diagonal.

4. Arrange squares on the fusible webbing, using the iron to attach according the manufacturers instructions. Cut the pieces from the webbing. *Note: Alternatively, you can and use a fabric glue stick to secure the onto the wool square.*

5. Place the pieces on the 16" wool square, leaving ⅛" or consistent spacing between each piece. Use a ruler to make certain the pattern is square and to help make certain the vertical and horizontal rows are straight and level with one another.

6. When satisfied with design, remove the backing from each of the fusible webbing pieces. Iron the pieces onto the wool. *Note: If using glue to attach, apply an even amount and press into place to set.*

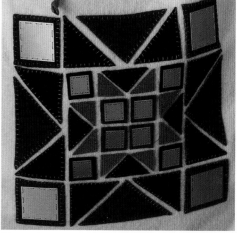

Photo 1

7. Edge the large exterior pieces all the way around each piece with a buttonhole stitch. Refer to Buttonhole Stitch on page 14. On the interior pieces, use a straight stitch to accent except where the tin pieces are used. Refer to Straight Stitch on page 15.

8. Stitch the tin pieces onto the fabric through the holes in the tin itself. *Note: If using pearl cotton, use a single strand. If using regular-weight thread, use two strands.* (Photo 1 and Photo 2)

Photo 1

Photo 2

INSTRUCTIONS FOR TOTE

Note: Use a ⅝" seam allowance on all seams.

1. Cut the following pieces from windowpane-patterned fabric for the outside of the tote:
   - 16" square for the outside back
   - three 4¾" x 16" pieces for the two side and bottom pieces
   - two 2½" x 24" strips for two piece handles

2. Cut the following pieces from the floral print fabric for the inside of the tote:
   - two 16" squares for front and back lining pieces
   - three 4¾" x 16" pieces for two sides and bottom piece
   - 10" x 20" piece for large pocket on front inside lining piece
   - 5" x 10" piece for back inside lining pocket
   - 5" x 18" piece for back inside lining
   - two 3" x 6" pieces for handle tabs to hold metal ring that will hold the handles
   - two 1½" x 18" strips for closure ties
   - 2" x 5" strip for key holder strap
   - two 2" x 24" strip for two piece handle

3. Sew the back and the two side pieces together. With the side pieces on opposite sides of the large square, press each seam facing into the side panel.

4. Sew the wool quilt front piece to the unsewn sides of the windowpane-pattern side pieces.

5. With the front, back, and side pieces sewn together, the right sides facing each other, pin the bottom windowpane piece in place. Sew around each edge. Trim corners to eliminate bulk. Turn right sides out.

6. Mark 1" down from the top edge at the center on the front and back on the outside pieces of the tote. *Note: This is where the closure ties will be attached.*

7. Fold each 1½" x 18" closure tie lengthwise with the right sides facing. Sew down each long edge, creating a tube. Use a turning tool or safety pin, turn the right sides facing out. Press the tube flat with the seam centered on the back of each tie. Push ½"–¾" of one end of the tie fabric back inside each tube. See Diagram A below. Tie a slip knot to hold this end closed. Slip-stitch the unfinished edges of the ties onto the front and back center of the tote, where it is marked. Refer to Slip Stitch on page 14. Stitch the two 1" tin squares to cover where you attached each tie. *Note: This will cover the cut edges.* (Photo 3)

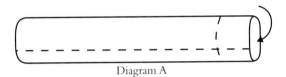
Diagram A

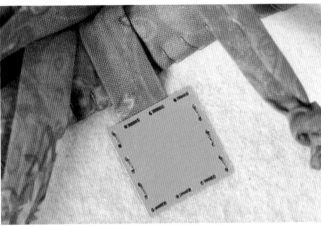
Photo 3

8. Adhere fusible interfacing to each lining piece and pocket piece. *Note: You will only need to cut the interfacing to cover one half of each pocket because they will be folded over.*

9. To sew the lining, follow the same method used in Steps 3–6 on page 56, except before sewing the two large square lining pieces to the side pieces, make and attach the pockets to the front and back lining pieces. *Note: This will eliminate the difficulty of working in a tight space created when all the sides are sewn.*

10. To make the pockets, fold the 10" x 20" back panel pocket piece in half lengthwise, with right sides together for a 10" square. Sew around the edges, leaving a 2" opening along one side. Repeat with the 5" x 10" piece and the 5" x 18" piece. Turn the pockets right side out through the 2" opening, making certain the corners and each seam are fully pushed out. Turn in the edges of the openings even with the other edges. Press flat and sew each pocket to either large side lining piece, stitching around the sides and the bottom. *Note: You can configure the pockets to fit the needs and the usage of the tote. They can be made long and narrow for pens and pencils or wide for pattern books.*

11. Cut the plastic canvas into two 4" x 16" pieces. Lay both pieces together into the bottom of the tote. *Note: This will reinforce the bottom of the bag and secure the edges of the two canvas pieces by handstitching through the openings of the canvas in several places to the side bottom seams of the tote.*

12. Insert the lining into the tote and adjust to fit well if necessary. Take several hidden stitches on each side at the bottom seams, catching both the lining and the outside together to hold the lining in place.

13. Fold the top of the lining over evenly to the outside of the tote. Tuck ¼" of the lining under to form a finished edge. Pin into place and topstitch with a coordinating thread around this edge either with a machine or by hand. Slip-stitch or buttonhole-stitch as desired. (Photo 4)

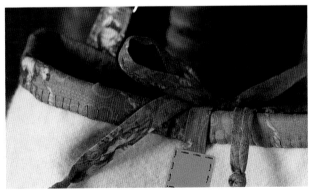
Photo 4

14. Press the 3" x 6" tab pieces in half lengthwise, right side out, folding ¼" in on each side.

15. Insert one end of the strip (tab) just completed through the rectangular metal ring, centering the ring in the middle of the strip at the fold. Machine-sew or hand-sew, up one side of the strip, and across just underneath the ring and down the other side. See Diagram B below. Zigzag-stitch the raw edge. Refer to Zigzag Stitch on page 15.

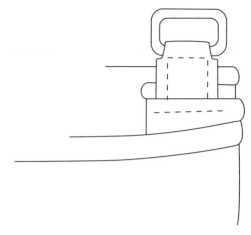

Diagram C

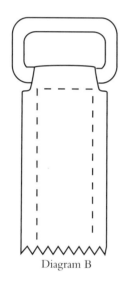

Diagram B

16. Insert the ring tabs at the tote opening into a fold, created by pinching the two side seams together with the fold facing to the inside of the tote. Center each tab into the inside of each fold made on either side of tote. Sew this "sandwich" of front, back, and tab pieces together by sewing a straight stitch across the tab. Refer to Straight Stitch on page 15. Backstitch several times to secure. To do this, pull the inside fold, which contains the tab, up and out far enough to fit it under the machine needle and stitch the tab width. Or you could turn the bag inside out and sew it. Make certain not to sew the front and back of purse in this sandwich, just the fold. See Diagram C at right. *Notes: The tabs fit only into the side panels of the purse. The key tab can be sewn on the inside where one of the handle tabs is sewn.*

17. Sew the 2" x 5" key holder piece in the same manner as the handle tabs in Steps 14–15 at left. Insert a key ring or clip instead of the rectangular ring into the fold, then attach where desired.

18. *Note: The handles have a slight variation to them in that they are made up of two straps that loop through each other, then join at each side tab.* For the two handles, sew a windowpane strip 1½" x 24" and a floral strip 1½" x 24" right sides together and turn right side out. Repeat again with remaining 12" x 24" pieces. Press flat, with seams on the outside edges. *Note: A different fabric is facing out on each side.*

19. Thread one end of the first strap through the ring on the tab at one side of the purse. *Note: This strap will have the floral lining side facing out.* Join both the ends of this piece together, making certain you have not twisted the strap. Pull the ends up with right side facing in. Stitch across ends to secure together. Turn the floral side out once again. *Note: The stitched ends will be enclosed between the two sides and will face in.*

19. Center the seamed end along the rectangular ring. Tuck any excess fabric into the center to get a good fit. Sew across the strap just above the top of the ring. *Note: The seam will be on the inside hidden by the ring edges.* (Photo 5)

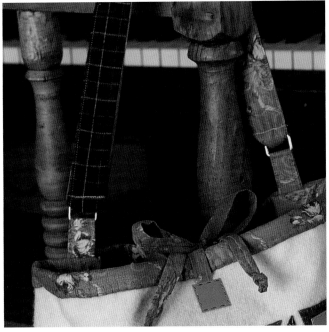

Photo 5

20. Loop one end of the second strap through the first strap and attach both ends to the other side rectangle held by the tabs inserted in Step 15, making certain the windowpane fabric is facing out. See Diagram D below.

Diagram D

21. Insert one end of first strap through the rectangular ring. Match it up with the other end of the same piece. Sewing in the same manner as the other strap in Steps 18–19 on pages 58–59. (Photo 6) *Note: You can machine-sew or hand-sew the tote sides together on the outside top edges with a few stitches. This will add stability to the shape and make the purse look a little leaner.*

Photo 6

Variations:

Chose different cottons, oilcloth, clear plastic to cover cloth, different colors, etc. The handle could be made of ribbon and strapping fabric. Adapt the pockets to hold anything in different shapes and sizes. Just be consistent with the seams and the measurements. You can vary the sizes and lengths as desired, long and narrow for knitting needles, wider for a rotary cutter. If you were to use this as a diaper bag, the pockets can be cut to fit a bottle, diapers, burp cloths, etc. Interface the pockets to desired thickness and use.

QUILT BLOCK PURSE

Have you ever passed a ready-made purse or bag and thought about how easily it would be to make it look so much better? Well, do it! This is an example of an inexpensive purse that is covered by wool, buttons, and a little glue. It certainly looks better and was a lot of fun to make. Maybe this is the bag you put your quilt patterns in, or a clipping from a magazine, when you go to a fabric store. There is enough room in the bag to put fat quarters in and all sorts of other items. It also could be used for anything else you wanted—it's plastic lined, how about the beach?

ITEMS TO GATHER

- General Items on page 10
- Wools:
    10" sq. beige
    dark cranberry for quilt block
    gold for quilt block
    light rust quilt block
    medium rust quilt block
- Purchased purse
- Wooden buttons

INSTRUCTIONS

1. Cut four 1½" squares from dark cranberry. Cut each in half.

2. Cut four ¾" squares and one 1½" square from light rust wool.

3. Cut four 1½" squares two 2" squares, and four ¾" squares from gold wool. Cut 2" squares and ¾" squares in half diagonally.

4. Cut two 1" squares from medium rust wool. Cut squares in half diagonally.

5. Beginning at the center, place the quilt pieces onto the beige square. Leave about ⅛" between each piece. *Note: Check frequently to ensure the pieces are square with the edges of the beige wool piece. If desired, you can butt the quilt pieces together. See Quilt Block Diagram below.*

Quilt Block Diagram

Photo 1

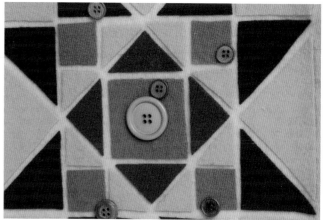

Photo 2

Photo 3

6. When satisfied with the placement of the quilt block, lift each piece one at a time and apply fabric glue, then replace it, checking that you are still in proper alignment. Press each piece firmly down to secure. Remove any excess glue before it dries. (Photo 1)

7. Glue the beige square onto the front of the purse. Lay a piece of plastic over the square and place a heavy object over the purse. Allow to dry. Glue each button firmly in place, starting on quilt block design. (Photo 2)

8. Glue remaining buttons onto purse. (Photo 3) Check the buttons to make certain they are securely attached, if not apply additional glue.

Helpful Suggestions:

Please watch young children around this purse; the buttons should not come off, but with kids anything is possible.

NINE PATCH HEART PANEL

NINE PATCH HEART PANEL

This is a collection of hearts cut from assorted wool patterns: plaids, herringbone, houndstooth, and tweed. They are attached to the red 2½" wool squares, then sewn onto an unusual color of wool. The wool is actually a scrap of wool felt from our much used pool table, yes it was pink. This is a great project for any skill and interest level. The fun part of this project as it is shown here, is the variety of stitches used and the different beads, buttons, and charms. As a sewing-machine project, can you imagine the variety of stitches you can use and the fun cords and threads that can be added?

ITEMS TO GATHER

- General Items on page 10
- Wools:
  2½" sq. red (9)
  14" sq. pink for background
- Assorted beads; buttons; charms
- Assorted fabric scraps
- Frame (optional)
- Threads: assorted; gray

INSTRUCTIONS

1. Photocopy Heart Pattern on page 116. *Note: If desired, pattern can be traced directly from book with tracing paper.* Cut out nine hearts from fabric scraps.

2. Glue one heart onto each red square. (Photo 1)

Photo 1

3. Stitch beads, buttons, and charms onto each heart. (Photo 2)

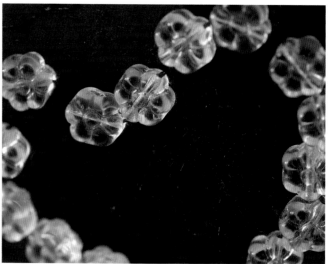

Photo 2

Photo 3

4. Lay out the square patch out on the background fabric as desired. (Photo 3)

5. When satisfied with arrangement, glue or pin and stitch squares into place on backing fabric.

6. Using desired stitch, stitch around each square. (Photo 4)

7. Frame as desired.

Helpful Suggestions:

This project was stretched across an acid-free backing and framed with a simple flat frame that was base-coated with paint, then sponged. The beauty of painting your own frame is the ease in which you can change the colors when you get in the mood to adjust.

Photo 4

HEART EMBELLISHED JACKET

I have always loved hearts and loved jackets with embellishments, so this is my wearable creation. You can use any style jacket. I found a hooded black denim jacket that I thought would provide a great background. Notice the features of the jacket to see how you might accent already present details. You can accent the front pockets, sleeves, back panel, etc.

ITEMS TO GATHER

- General Items on page 10
- Wools:
  herringbone
  red felt
- 2" sq. cardboard
- Fusible interfacing
- Printer paper
- Purchased jacket
- Red heart buttons (3)
- Red metallic cord
- Threads: assorted; red metallic

INSTRUCTIONS

1. Use a square piece of paper to determine the size of patch for the jacket back. If necessary, cut paper to desired size.

2. Enlarge or reduce and photocopy Heart Jacket Pattern on page 116 as desired to fit onto the paper patch. When satisfied with both of the pieces, the heart and the patch, cut heart from red felt and fusible interfacing.

3. Cut the square patch from herringbone wool, adding ½" to each side to fold under for a finished edge.

4. Place the square on the back of the jacket and pin in place. Try the jacket on to make certain the placement is correct and level. Mark the placement with pins. Remove the square. Center and pin the heart onto square.

5. Fuse the red heart to the herringbone square, following interfacing manufacturer's instructions.

6. Outline the red heart with the cord, using a zigzag-stitch and matching thread. Refer to Zigzag Stitch on page 15. Zigzag stitch several times around the heart, even going out beyond the edges.

7. Make a small tassel by wrapping thread or cord around 2" square of cardboard. enough times to make the desired tassel fullness.

8. Slide a length of thread through the top loops of the thread and knot. Carefully slide the thread off the cardboard. Tie the loop top together, then wrap the thread around several times, a short distance below the top of the tassel and tie off. Sew the tassel either by hand or machine just at the bottom of the heart.

9. Press the edges of wool patch square under. Place the square back onto the jacket as indicated by your pins; try it on to make certain of placement.

10. Topstitch in place with matching threads. Remove pins. (Photo 1)

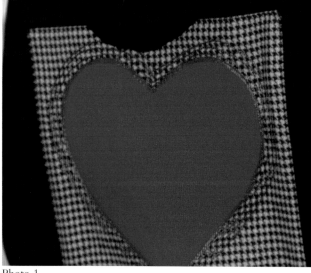
Photo 1

11. Measure the circumference of the cuff, adding about 1". Cut three strips 1¼" wide by measurement length from herringbone wool. Iron the raw edges of the wool strip to the wrong side ¼" on each side.

12. Place each strip on the jacket cuff. Pin in place, overlapping the ends at the sleeve seam line to have an overlap of about ¼".

13. Turn the one edge of the strip under to cover the other end and pin in place.

14. Topstitch over each side of this band. Zigzag stitch again with metallic thread. Remove the pins. (Photo 2)

Photo 2

15. Sew remaining band by placing it along the yolk seam of the chest and on the inside of the jacket. Zigzag-stitch band with metallic thread. (Photo 3)

Photo 3

16. Stitch buttons onto band to accent.

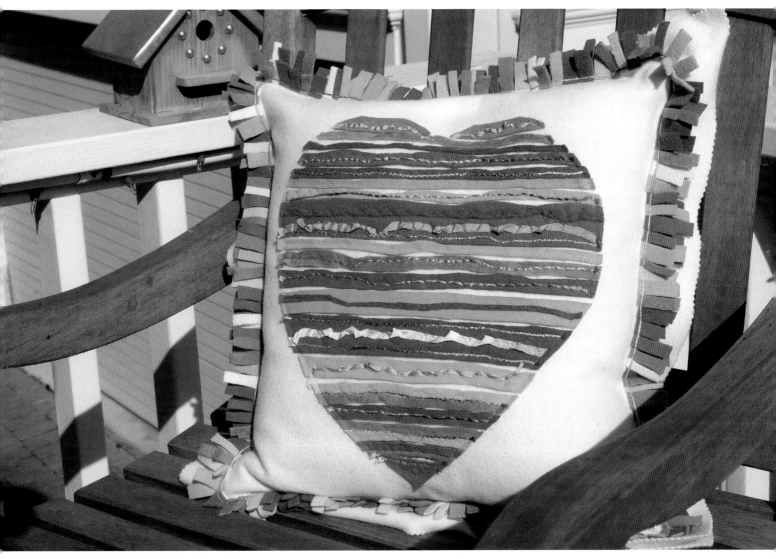

ITEMS TO GATHER

- General Items on page 10
- Wools:
  20" sq. cream (2)
  assorted scraps
- 16" pillow form
- Assorted fibers; ribbons
- Pinking shears
- Threads: assorted; cream; monofilament
- Transparent tape

This is a fun pillow to make and the perfect project for any skill level because you can make it as simple or elaborate as you like. For the project shown, I used a sewing machine, a paper pattern, and pins. You could use fusible interfacing, fabric glue and/or assorted threads and beads.

INSTRUCTIONS

1. Enlarge 200% and photocopy Wool Heart Pillow Pattern on page 116. Place heart pattern in the center of one cream square, securing with just enough tape to hold in place.

2. Using fabric shears and pinking shears, cut strips from wool, fibers, and ribbon. Lay strips across the paper heart pattern, varying the size and color of the embellishments until satisfied with look of heart.

3. Trim the strips to just overlap the edge of the paper heart pattern underneath by ½".

4. Pin or tape the overlapping strip edges down one side of the fabric heart.

5. Gently remove the paper heart pattern and rearrange any strips that have been disturbed. *Note: You now have a heart pattern that is shaped by horizontal strips.* Add additional embellishments at this stage.

6. Pin all strips into place and carefully secure the pieces with fabric glue. Attach the pieces using one of the following methods:

   a. If gluing, apply enough to secure it well, making certain that the glue is well hidden. (Photo 1)

Photo 1

   b. If sewing, apply a small amount of liquid fabric glue, glue stick, or pin to secure in place while you work. If machine-sewing, drop the feed dogs and use free-motion-sewing. Stitch around the edges of the heart along each piece of wool, ribbon, and fiber. (Photo 2)

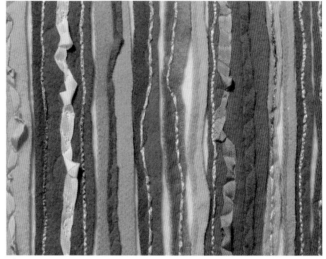
Photo 2

7. Cut numerous ½" x 3" strips from wool scraps for border. *Note: This measurement can vary to add variety to the fringe border.* (Photo 3)

Photo 3

8. Using a fabric marker, draw a 2" border line in from the front square edge.

9. Pin and center the strips, one at a time, across the drawn line, varying the colors as they are sewn. (Photo 4)

Photo 4

10. At the corners, overlap the strips to form a tight curve and continue on around the square. (Photo 5)

Photo 5

11. Fold and press the fringe pieces toward the outside edges. Using one of the decorative fibers and the machine-zigzag, stitch around on the folded edge. (Photo 6)

Photo 6

12. Place the two 20" wool squares together, with the heart facing out.

13. Align the front square edges with the back square edges. Sew together just to the inside of the folded fringe. Leave a 12" opening on one side.

14. Insert pillow form into the opening and pin. Stitch opening closed. Remove pins.

Variations:

The foundation colors can be more subtle or very dramatic. Change the shape or size of heart. Use more free-motion-sewing around or on the heart, into the open space. Embellish the back of the pillow. Stitch jewels and beads on strips. For those who wish to just use adhesives, wool strips can be applied with fusible interfacing and the fibers and ribbons can be applied with fabric glue. The pillow can be attached with fusible tape. The pillow can be made as simple or as complicated as you wish.

HEART PHOTO ALBUM

This project was made from a plain photo album and covered with a soft suede leather, then black/white fabric hearts edged with beads were added. The instructions for this project can be easily adapted to any size binder or book. The embellishments and fabric choices can vary greatly. You have the opportunity to be formal or funky. Remember that if the photo album has a specific direction to it you will need to lay out your pattern to honor this. It would be a shame to have all your photos fall out because the loading end was not right side up.

ITEMS TO GATHER

- General Items on page 10
- Black/white fabric scraps
- Bugle beads
- Double-sided adhesive sheet
- Heavy-weight decorative paper or fabric-wrapped lightweight cardboard/cardstock
- Photo album
- Red suede leather, cut 1" larger all around then entire outside of album
- Rubber cement
- Tweezers

INSTRUCTIONS

1. Using craft scissors, cut the adhesive sheet to fit the front, back, and spine of the album. *Note: This can be done one side at a time or all at once.*

2. Apply adhesive sheet to the front, spine and back of the album, leaving the outside protective backing attached.

3. Lay the leather flat. Peel of the protective sheet from the front of the album and carefully center press firmly in place.

4. Repeat the Step 3 above for the album spine and back.

5. Cut the adhesive strips to fit the inside the edges of the album cover. Adhere the strips, leaving the outside protective backing attached.

6. Trim the edges of the leather as shown in the Album Diagram below. Remove the protective outside backing one strip at a time and fold the leather over to inside cover.

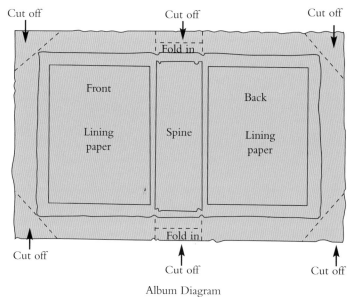

Album Diagram

7. Tuck leather under the binding or ring mechanism, trimming excess if necessary. (Photo 1)

Photo 1

8. Cut the heavy decorative paper large enough to overlap the leather that has been brought around from the front. Apply rubber cement to the paper and lay in place.

9. Freehand-cut nine hearts from the black/white fabric.

10. Trace the heart shapes onto the adhesive sheets, leaving enough space around each heart to cut ⅛" larger than the fabric heart.

11. Cut hearts from adhesive sheets ⅛" larger than drawn. Center and apply the fabric hearts to adhesive hearts.

12. Arrange the hearts as desired being careful of the uncovered adhesive edges. When satisfied with design, remove the protective backing from the hearts and secure in place. (Photo 2)

Photo 2

13. Using a pair of tweezers, place bugle beads around each heart. *Note: The uncovered adhesive edge keeps the beads in place.* (Photo 3)

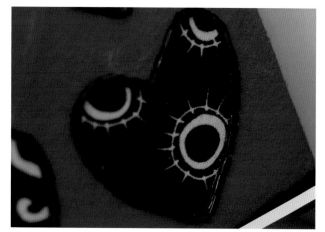

Photo 3

14. When satisfied with design, apply a small bead of clear glue around the inside of the beading to secure.

HOME SWEET HOME

SEASIDE TRIO

This is truly a scrap-stash project. The buildings along the seashore are so colorful, the atmosphere, especially on a vacation, is almost unbelievable. This is a tiny rendition of those feelings. Buttons instead of palms, beads and bit of chipped gem stones, pieces of real coral and a few shells, golden sea creatures, a purple button that looks like brain coral—sort of. Let's begin.

ITEMS TO GATHER

- General Items on page 10
- Wools:
  12" sq. light blue
  12"–13" strips: cream; true blue; gold; turquoise
  16" sq. gold wool
  bright colored scraps
- ⅛" x 18" dowels (4)
- 2" dia. brass sun
- 16" acid-free foam-core board
- 20-gauge wire (5")
- Assorted embellishments: beads; buttons; shells
- Glue dots
- Micro-beads: blue; gold; silver
- Wire cutters

INSTRUCTIONS

1. Center and glue 12" blue wool square onto 16" gold wool square.

2. Freehand-cut out three buildings from desired wools. Center and place buildings approximately 5" above the bottom edge of the blue wool.

3. Freehand-cut out the separate windows, doors, and roofs from desired wools. Place onto the building shapes as desired.

4. Glue all items in place once satisfied.

5. Freehand-cut the tree trunks and bushes from desired wools. Glue in place.

6. Glue wool strips in place for sand, water, and sky, making certain they are as horizontal as possible. (Photo 1)

Photo 1

7. Embellish as desired with beads, buttons, and shells, using adhesive dots. Use clear craft glue to attach the micro-beads and basically everything that is too small for the adhesive dots. *Note: Use the adhesive dots for items large enough to hide them.* (Photo 2)

Photo 2

8. Attach sun with a ring of adhesive dots. Allow the dots to extend beyond the center of the sun and pour gold micro beads around the edges. *Note: Use tweezers to help if needed.* (Photo 3)

Photo 3

9. Mount onto foam-core board. Attach dowels to the top and bottom. *Note: These dowels were painted to coordinate with the project. The weight of the bottom dowels, keep the project flat.* (Photo 4)

Photo 4

10. Insert a 6" length of wire through the wool from the center back point, corresponding with the top dowel. Wrap wire around dowel three times. Push wire out through the wool to the back. Twist the end together, forming a loop for a hanger.

Helpful Suggestions:

Hang small shells and starfish from the bottom of the gold backing. Instead of buttons, use fancy beads or sew coral twigs across the bottom and all around the blue square, Freehand-cut fish, palm fronds, seashells, etc. This would also be a successful sewing project. Can you imagine all the fun fibers and threads that could be sewn on with a variety of stitches?

YOUR HOME IN A TAPESTRY

Many of us have lived or will live in more than one home, oftentimes a lot more. Each home holds memories for us that make it special. The feeling you have for certain homes can affect how you envision the home and influence how you render it in any medium. I will tell you how I went about moving this little cottage from film to finish so that you can do the same with your own home.

ITEMS TO GATHER

- General Items on page 10
- Wools:
  assorted scraps
- Coordinating fabric larger all around than finished piece for decorative backing
- Foam-core board topped with acid-free mat board
- Graph paper
- Lightbox or window
- Photocopier or scanner
- Photograph of house
- Ruler
- Tracing paper
- Tweezers

Note: If possible, take photographs of your project from several angles. Notice the angles that are seen in the picture—is the house showing the side of the roof and exterior walls, can you see enough of the detail of the house, is it covered with bushes? How much detail do you want to include in your project. Are there enough colors to provide a contrast in the features of the home? There are a lot of things to consider.

This is a wonderful old home with history and character. The photo looks fairly simple and yet there is a stroller on the porch, glass bricks around the front door, a trellis between the two front windows, a lovely birdbath, honeysuckle vines, lavender, butterfly bushes, a great white pyramid, roses, fruit trees, boxwood, and amazing monkey puzzle tree—a lot to include for this medium of wool, fibers, and glue. Choose the details to include, those to eliminate. and how much liberty can you take in moving things just a little to make this project work.

INSTRUCTIONS

1. Enlarge original photo to several different sizes on photocopier or scanner. Review each copy for that which shows what you want and is closest to your working project goal.

2. Using a lightbox or a window, draw the house and its surrounding features onto tracing paper.

3. Compare this tracing with the photo and enlargements and see what you want to emphasize. *Note: I like the tall narrowness of the house and the way it fit so snugly in the yard. I loved the white picket fence and I loved the monkey-puzzle tree. The birdbath didn't show up well, the stroller covered the glass bricks, the white pyramid was too delicate to include effectively and the monkey-puzzle tree was just not working in the drawing—too far out of my focus area. So, those few features were eliminated for now.*

4. Draw the main pieces on graph paper. *Note: I decided I didn't want to deal with the side view so I made the house face full front. I needed the color of the roof so I showed it as an edge feature (first inaccuracy). The windows I drew fit the house I was drawing, yet weren't exactly like the original house (second inaccuracy). You can rework your drawings or simply move on and see how things come out.*

Photo 1

Photo 2

Photo 3

5. Find and choose the colors you can work with. *Note: Since the house is green and so are the trees and grass, I had to think about what greens to use and how to place them so that they wouldn't blend with each other.*

6. Take measurements from drawings on graph paper and cut the pieces that way or cut up drawing. Lay each piece on the background fabric, working from the large pieces to the small pieces. Step back and look at it. *Note: Are you off square? That will drive you crazy unless the house is that way originally.* Using a ruler, straighten things out if necessary. Layer each section and piece. When you have a sound arrangement with the larger pieces, glue them down lightly if you are hand- or machine-sewing. Glue down more securely if you are only gluing this project.

7. Begin to add detail. (Photo 1, Photo 2, Photo 3) *Note: The wooden siding has delightful horizontal shadows. I didn't do the siding with individual strips; I used a solid background and added long slivers of a shadow fabric and placed those on. The windows all looked different. The upper one was pale, the one on the left had a shade down, and the one on the right showed the interior. I didn't want a lot of detail there except the basics and those great lampshades—good color. I added shadow details on the windows and the roof to hint at dimension, but didn't get carried away with small detail because I knew I wasn't doing any hand- or machine-sewing on this. If I do this house again, I will very likely do a lot of handwork, adding the stroller and the flowers—especially those between the windows on the trellis. Tweezers come in quite handy with all the small strips and pieces.*

Photo 4

8. Layer the house and its backing onto two other coordinating fabrics. (Photo 4)

9. Mount finished project onto foam-core board.

Helpful Suggestions:

The home isn't 100% accurate but the feel of it is sufficient to stir memories. You will very likely want to do this project again—stretching your abilities and increasing points of interest that will work well. You can always make changes and alter what you see and what you do to suit your skills and interests. This project can be framed, hung on the wall as it is, turned into a pillow, or made into one of the blocks of your home-show quilt project by changing the fabric.

FAMILY GAME BOX

The next time you go to your favorite "deal" store, look for a sturdy wooden box that would be perfect for holding your smaller game "stuff": decks of cards, bingo pieces, dice. The box can have a hinged or lift-off lid. Whether it is attractive or not, you can change it to be your new game box with this fun idea. The top and outsides of the box are covered with the green wool and a scattering of shapes: squares, triangles, curls, bars, and circles cut from scraps.

ITEMS TO GATHER

- General Items on page 10
- Wools:
  assorted scraps
  felt, sufficient to cover outside of box
  felt, sufficient to line inside of box
- 1" dice pieces (4 pkgs or 20 pieces)
- Craft knife or sandpaper
- Decorative paper for lining (optional)
- Graph paper
- Industrial-strength glue
- Quilt batting (optional)
- Ruler
- Screwdriver to remove hardware
- Tear-away paper
- Weights (optional)
- Wooden box

Note: Look at the box you have just acquired, see how it is covered, top and bottom, sides and lid. Learn from this and see if you want to follow its example. The contents that will be stored in the box can help you with the outside design. Cards, bingo, word games, or dice can all be adapted to simple designs for the outside of the box. Play around with ideas on scratch paper as you plan the design. The inside of this box was originally covered with paper, as well as the outside bottom. You can duplicate this with a heavy paper that has wonderful prints or patterns to complement your outside fabric colors, or you can line the inside and lid with fabric that matches, contrasts, or accents the outside design. Lay the outside fabric down and play with the scraps to see what colors go with it and each other.

INSTRUCTIONS

1. Remove the lid hinges and any other hardware if present and set aside. If there are any braids or trims, carefully remove them.

2. Evaluate the smoothness of the covering. Check for any problems such as ridges, globs of glue, etc., that may show through the fabric when recovering it. Smooth out the problems by trimming them with a craft knife or sandpaper. *Note: If they are still noticeable, cover the box with a layer of quilt batting before covering with decorative fabric.*

3. To begin, measure the side of the box, adding ½" seam allowance wherever necessary to accommodate seams. Cut from wool. *Note: You may not have a single piece of wool large enough to go all the way around the box. Seam where necessary to obtain the length necessary.*

4. Measure the height of the box side adding ½" overlap to the bottom measurement and at least 1" overlap into the inside of the box at the top. Cut from wool.

5. For the inside measurements, add any seaming necessary. *Note: Since we are using wool on the inside, the seams will simply butt up to each other and not overlap—a flat transition along the walls. The wool on the outside needs sewn seams for strength.* Cut from wool.

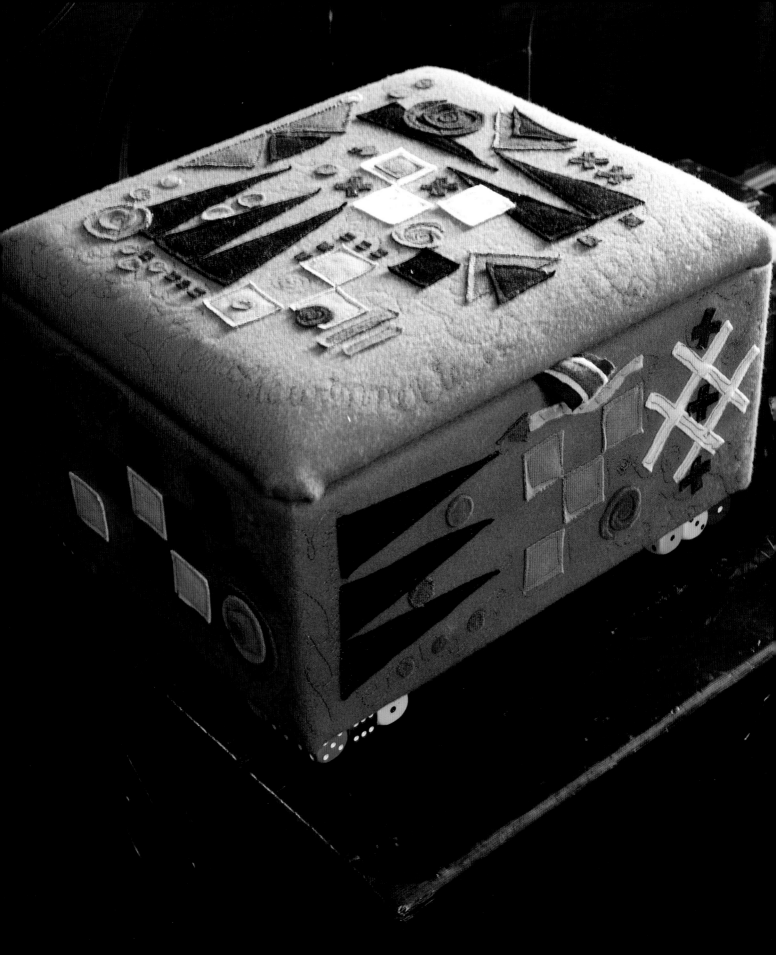

6. Measure the lid by going from one edge, across the curve of the top and down to the other side, then add 1" to the measurement on all sides. Cut from wool. *Note: The extra 1" will be wrapped around the lid to the underside of the lid to provide good coverage.*

7. Measure the inside of the lid ½" smaller than the actual flat measurement. Cut from wool. *Note: This piece of fabric will cover the wrap around created from the top fabric of the lid.*

8. Freehand-cut desired shapes from wool scraps. Draw box and lid shapes on graph paper. Lay out the design on paper. *Note: Remember the placement will be affected by the wrapping of the fabric around the edges of the lid and the box side, top, and bottom.* (Photo 1)

Photo 1

9. When satisfied with design, place shapes onto cut wool pieces. Attach pieces, using one of the following methods:

   a. For an all-glue project, attach each piece before placing the fabric on the box. Glue carefully and try to make certain that there is no glue showing beyond each piece. Place weights over the fabric to encourage a flat and secure bond.

   b. For a hand-stitched project, glue pieces down lightly. Allow to dry. Stitch as desired, using fun outline stitches, satin stitching, and contrasting colors for thread.

   c. For machine-sewing, glue each piece lightly in place, and allow to dry. If necessary, secure more firmly with pins. Use dropped feed dogs on the machine. Sew around and between each piece. *Note: This need not be overwhelming. A great way to practice your freehand-sewing skills is to use an old unthreaded needle and piece of paper and start sewing. The paper is a little easier to move about but will give you a chance to get use to this skill. You will find that you can write and draw with the needle, add thread and you have a great project.*

10. If desired, cut and place pieces of tracing paper or tear-away paper to fit in between the designs. Using a pencil, write "bingo," "and the winner is…" or any fun game lingo or designs on paper pieces. Pin into place. Sew over the designs, then tear away the paper.

11. Wrap the finished cover around the box lid and pin temporarily in place.

12. Adjust the placement of the top fabric and re-pin. Turn the lid over and begin to glue each side down by running a line of glue along the outside edge of the fabric. Smooth glue to the flat inside part of the lid. Pin every 1" or so, slanting the pinhead away from the fabric, just catching about a ¼" of the fabric. Avoid pulling the wool so tight that it is distorted. *Note: The pin holds the edge in place but doesn't pull it into a wavy line.*

13. At the corners, trim excess fabric to lessen the bulk.

14. Fold the sides over the corner and pin in place. Glue and allow to dry. Remove pins.

15. Cut a piece of wool to fit the inside top and size it approximately ½" smaller than lid, but large enough to be certain the edges of the outside top fabric are covered. Glue and pin into place. Allow to dry.

16. Cut one 1½" x 6" piece, one ¾" x 6" piece, and one ½" x 6" piece for handle. Center and glue the ½" piece onto ¾" piece. Center and glue the ¾" piece onto 1½" piece. When dry, fold in half, stitch to the lining fabric or glue into place for handle.

17. Wrap the embellished fabric around the box sides, fitting the fabric so that there is about ½" overlap of fabric on the bottom and enough fabric on the top to wrap up over the side and into the box.

18. Remove the fabric from the box and sew the final edge together. If gluing the project, proceed. Reposition the fabric around the side edges of the box.

19. Cover the box bottom, following the Step 15 above.

20. Line the inside of the box with individual pieces of wool or fabric. Glue into place. (Photo 2)

21. Turn the box on its top and attach the five dice at each corner, one dice at each corner and two on each side. Glue the dice to the box and each other. Allow to dry.

22. Reattach the lid hinges and any other hardware.

Variations:

Try a ready-quilted fabric, silk, or leather. This can also be very a chic or rambunctious box. For a handle, use a large bead, a wooden or brass door pull, or a small purse handle made of bamboo. The insides can be covered with playing cards, instruction sheets, road maps, photos, or any wrapping paper or fabric that you choose. Different legs can be added to this box by using brass door pulls, glass knobs, painted wooden blocks, or old spools of thread if you were doing a sewing box.

Photo 2

TREASURE CHEST

This chest is a great place to store the remote control, crossword puzzles, books, and magazines when they are not being used. It is a giant version of our Family Game Box on page 82. It is covered in the same manner with a slight difference. Each corner of the box is accented by a triangle that is sewn on as a design element. The decorative cord and unusual beads as accent pieces are also variations of the Family Game Box. Use a box you have at home or go hunting for the perfect one to redo.

ITEMS TO GATHER

- General Items on page 10
- Wools:
  light gold (1 yd)
  light yellow (¼ yd)
- Assorted stone and semi-precious beads
- Flat and round brass discs
- Large clips/clamps
- Lining fabric-cotton print (1 yd)
- Medium-weight acid-free mat board to fit the inside, outside, and bottom of the chest
- Ruler
- Threads: assorted; invisible; yellow/gold
- Wool fiber cords: variegated fiber (1 ball); yellow/gold fiber (1 ball)
- Wooden box

Note: Please carefully read the instructions given with the Family Game Box project on pages 82–85. All sewing for the outside wool cover is done before the wool is attached to the box. You can add other touches to the box after it is assembled and secured. It is easier to do any sewing before hand. The instructions found in the Family Game Box project are basically the same as for this large chest project. The measuring is the same. The gluing for the inside lining varies only if you are using a lighter weight fabric as we are in this specific design.

INSTRUCTIONS

1. Remove any hardware present on the box and set aside.

2. Measure and cut the chest sides from light gold wool. Refer Family Game Box Steps 1–3 on page 82. Before sewing up the final side seam, mark three horizontal lines the length of the fabric. *Note: The lines are intended to be evenly spaced horizontally on the side of the box—eliminate the overlapping measurements and set the lines in the center of the box's side.* Mark the vertical lines spaced the same width as the horizontal lines.

3. Measure and cut the chest top. Refer to Family Game Box, Steps 6–9 on page 84. Insert at each corner a 1¼"-wide strip of light yellow wool (the length will be determined by how far into the square you place the wool inset.) To do this cut off each corner of the outer lid wool, attach the light yellow wool inset to the main body of the wool, overlapping ⅛". Machine-topstitch this with a small zigzag stitch. Attach the previously removed corner pieces in the same way and trim the newly made square back down to the correct measurement. Refer to Family Game Box, Step 3 on page 82.

4. Cover the seams with decorative cord to accent the top. Sew up the side seam (seams) lining the horizontal lines up so that they match.

5. Machine-sew the decorative fibers onto the wool using cord foot. If you do not have a cording foot, use a small machine-zigzag stitch to sew over the fiber or hand-sew. Sew over the marked horizontal lines with the variegated fiber with invisible thread for all the machine sewing. Sew the vertical lines with the yellow gold fiber. *Note: These lines may wobble a little— no problem— this is handmade.*

6. Sew four spirals onto the lid fabric and other spirals to the side panel fabric. The spirals vary in size and shape and both the variegated and yellow gold fibers were used. (Photo 1)

Photo 1

7. Stitch the assorted beads onto the wool with sturdy yellow thread. *Note: I tried a few brass discs and found that some were so sharp that they thread was cut—consider the security of each bead as you sew. The large flat "donuts" are jade and also glass. Think of foot comfort when adding beads—more flat ones in the center top, more dimensional beads on the sides.*

8. Apply the sides and top fabric. Refer to Family Game Box, Steps 12–14 on pages 84–85.

9. Cut mat boards to fit each side wall of the inside box and the underside of the lid. *Note: I didn't cover the inside bottom because the color was a good accent color to the cotton print I was using. If you choose to cover the bottom measure as you would the other pieces.*

10. Cut the lining fabric so that it overlaps each mat board piece ½"–1" on all sides with lining fabric. Glue fabric to one side of each mat board, then fully glue the other side of each piece to the matching inside panels of the box. Hold pieces in place with large clips until dried. Cover the lid lining with fabric and glue in the same manner and hold in place by pins that pierced the edge of the fabric into the wood of the box. (Photo 2)

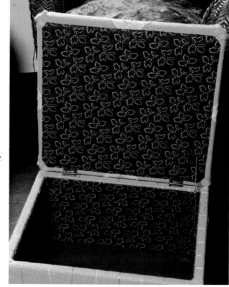

Photo 2

11. Measure and cut a piece of mat board to fit the outside bottom of the chest. The bottom piece can be left the color of the mat board or covered with fabric. *Note: If you have legs already attached to the bottom of the chest, cut out from the mat board the space needed for each leg.* Glue in place.

Variations:

Cover or paint the legs on the chest to match the final design. Appliqué pieces onto chest that coordinate with your home décor. Make a seasonal chest.

COZY FOOT STOOL

ITEMS TO GATHER

- General Items on page 10
- Wools:
  12" sq.: medium blue; brown; hand-dyed light gold;
  apple green; hand-dyed dark green; medium green;
  navy; pink; hand-dyed light rose; medium rose
  dark gold (1 yd)
- 40"-wide x 4"-thick foam (2)
- 8"-long wooden legs (4)
- 20" dia. pinewood circle (1)
- Acrylic paints
- Cotton muslin (1 yd)
- Craft knife or electric carving knife
- Drill/drill bits
- Flat plate metal leg holders/screws (4)
- Glue gun/glue sticks
- Light-colored cord (1 yd)
- Medium-loft quilt batting (1 yd)
- Paintbrush
- Screwdriver (optional)
- Staple gun

INSTRUCTIONS

Note: The wooden legs available for this project have a threaded post at one end that is screwed into a square metal receiving plate. The plate can be flat or have a slight angle to it. The legs would angle out slightly with these plates. The choice is yours as to which ones you use.

1. Using a pencil, mark the holes on the leg plates where the screws will go. Using an appropriate size drill-bit, drill the starter holes at each marked spot. Fasten the plate in position, using the drill with a screwdriver bit or a regular screwdriver.

2. Trace two pinewood circles onto each piece of foam. Using a craft knife or an electric carving knife, cut out the four foam circles. Turn the wooden circle over and glue on the foam rounds. Hot-glue the foam circles onto the pine circles, then to each other—making certain they are centered evenly over each other and the wooden base.

3. Cover the two layers of foam and the base with the medium-weight batting. To do this, place the batting evenly over the stool; gently pull the batting snugly over the foam and temporarily insert pins into the bottom layer of foam just above the wood. Even out the gathers that will occur. When satisfied, turn the stool over and trim the batting just long enough to cover the wooden base and about 1" beyond to the bottom side. Hot-glue the batting securely to the bottom.

4. Measure and cut a circle the diameter of the top of the stool from the muslin for a cover for the batting. For the side pieces, measure the height of the stool from the wooden base to the top. Add 1½" to that length for a seam allowance plus a fold-under length. Measure around the stool and add ½" for seam allowances. Cut the side material dimensions you have just measured. Test the side fabric to make certain you are accurate by pinning where the side seam will go—you want a snug fit but not so tight that it tears the batting when its pulled down.

5. Sew the side seam, then fit the round top into the side piece, right sides together, pinning into place. Sew the side and the top pieces together. Turn so that the seams face inside and slip the muslin cover over the stool. Either staple or glue the muslin edges to the base of the stools wooden circle, covering the batting that was previously glued down. *Note: By covering the batting with a muslin casing, it will allow you to wash or replace the outer covering without damaging the batting or foam.*

6. For the outside cover, measure as you did for the muslin cover in Step 4 above, adding 3" to the height of the side panel. Cut the pieces from the gold wool. Sew gold wool the same way you did the muslin cover in Step 5 above. Once cover has been sewn and tried on to check the fit, mark where the bottom of the stool meets the side material. Trim the

length of the sides even all around. Fold the bottom sides to the inside cover and pin in place just below where marked. Sew a double row of stitches ¼" inside the edge, leaving 1" opening at side seam. Run the cord through opening in side seam and around through the sewn casing. Pull both ends of the cord to the inside and use them to tighten the cover under the chair.

7. Photocopy Cozy Foot Stool Patterns on pages 117–119. *Note: If desired, patterns can be traced directly from book with tracing paper.* Cut patterns from 12" wool squares.

8. Freehand-cut stems. Place the flowers, leaves, and stems onto the stool. (Photo 1)

Photo 1

9. When satisfied with the design, glue or sew the flowers in place, using one of the following methods:

   a. If you plan to only glue the flowers in place, use a liquid fabric glue and cover the back of each piece well, then hold the pieces in place until dry. Double-check each piece to make certain it is glued down well. Use more glue if necessary.

   b. For a sewing project, glue each piece down just enough to hold it in place. Add a few pins, if necessary. If hand-sewing, stitch away. If machine-sewing, place clear thread in the top of the machine and a matching gold thread in the bobbin. Sew around each shape's edge as well as into the leaves and flowers to mimic veins and floral features. For the stems, zigzag across the stem rather than following its length. Stitch onto the gold background, making tendrils. For the grass, follow each blade up and down until reaching a stem, then proceed up the flower, sewing around each leaf or blossom and back down. Make certain to catch any blades of grass missed. When finished, place the cover on the stool and look carefully for petals or leaves not caught. Apply additional stitching, if desired. Check again. *Note: Use fray preventative on any edges that may begin to fray.*

10. Place the cover on the stool; pull the cord tight under the stool. Tie the ends and tuck them into the gathered fabric.

11. Paint the legs as desired. Allow to dry. (Photo 2)

Photo 2

Variations:

Add a skirt, choose different legs, or add shiny fabrics for some of the flowers. You also can stitch beads onto the flowers.

SEASONAL
SENSATIONS

SPOOKY WALL HANGING

ITEMS TO GATHER

- General Items on page 10
- Wools:
  ¼" x 19" light brown
  ½" x 19" cream (4)
  ¾" x 19" gold
  6" dia. hand-dyed gold circle for moon
  6" x 9" navy for house
  12" sq. dark gray for tree
  18" x 27" orange for backing
  assorted scraps: black; dark red; yellow
- ⅛" dia. wooden dowels (3)
- Assorted decorative fibers
- Assorted threads
- Cotton batting scraps
- Fall berry garland
- Gold stars with hole in center
- Tulle: 20" x 29" black; gray (scraps); teal (scraps)
- Wire cutters

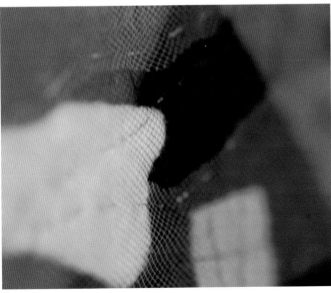

Photo 1

INSTRUCTIONS

1. Fringe top and bottom of the orange wool by carefully pulling out the horizontal threads ½"–¾" deep from the edge of the wool. *Note: This will become the backing.*

2. Enlarge as indicated and photocopy Spooky Wall Hanging Patterns on page 121. *Note: If desired, Bat and Small Tree pattern can be traced directly from book with tracing paper.* Cut the house from navy wool. Cut both trees from gray wool. Cut several bats from black wool.

3. Cut four 1" squares from the yellow scraps for windows. Cut one 1¼" x 2⅛" rectangle from red wool for door.

4. Freehand-cut the ghosts from the cotton batting scraps, stretching these shapes out a little to add a bit of thinning and irregularity to the shapes.

5. Cut long horizontal pieces from light brown, gold, and cream wools. Place the light brown band onto the wider gold band and glue to secure. Refer to photograph on page 93.

6. Position all the above pieces along with 6" gold circle for the moon on the orange backing as desired. Glue pieces down if you want this to be a nonsewing project. Or glue them just enough to be held into place until you sew them down later.

7. Lay the black tulle over the design and pin into place. (Photo 1) Cut and glue additional black tulle to fit over the three lower windows, covering one of them only halfway. *Note: This gives a variety of "light" coming from the house.*

8. Cut strips from tulle scraps to make the appearance of low clouds and fog. Place the gray strips, overlapping the tree and other pieces. (Photo 2) *Note: The strips are not uniform in any manner; they are just to suggest fog.* Place teal strips over some of the gray fog and have some stand alone. Add tulle strips as desired from the top and at the bottom across the house.

SPOOKY WALL HANGING

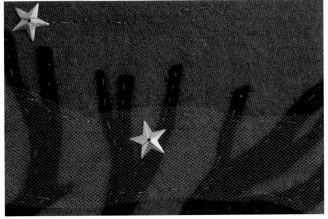

Photo 2

9. On top of the black tulle, place the bats and lay the decorative fibers between the horizontal lines. Pin in place. Tuck the stars on top of the black tulle and underneath the fog strips.

10. Using matching threads, sew the black tulle in place accenting stars, bats, and fog.

11. Lay the garland along the top of the design and down the right side until the desired look is achieved. (Photo 3)

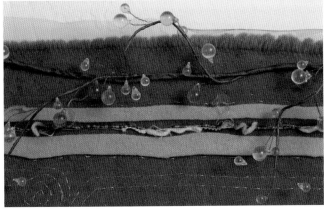

Photo 3

12. Trim the excess with wire cutters. Pin the garland in place. Glue the main wire at strategic places, holding each spot with a pin until it dries or use a needle and thread to catch the garland in place to ensure that it stays where you want it.

13. Once the garland is secure, bend and arrange the wires and tendrils as desired; but be certain to allow the hanging to be as flat as possible.

14. Cut two 1½" x 7" pieces from scrap wool. Place pieces onto the top back of the hanging, leaving about 2" open between the two pieces at the center at the center to allow a space from which to hang the wall hanging. Slip-stitch into place, or glue along the edges, top, and bottom, leaving the ends open. Refer to Slip Stitch on page 14.

15. When secure, insert the three dowels through the two pockets, allowing the excess to extend evenly on both sides.

16. Decide how far you want the dowels to extend from the hanging itself. Using the wire-cutters, cut each small dowel in varying lengths, creating the effect of twigs. *Note: For this project, the dowels extend about 2"–3" out on each side.*

17. Wind the garland around and through each stick to mimic the vine growth you might see along a fence. (Photo 4)

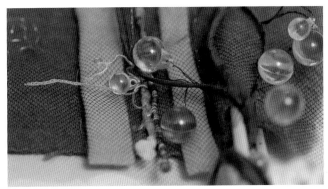

Photo 4

18. Use the exposed rods in the center of the back to hang the picture.

Variations:

The dowels can be replaced with twisted branches. Alter the house: lengthening it and enlarging the windows, adding a ghostly face or two peering out.

SNUGLY FALL BLANKET

This is a great project to work with on a chilly day when you need a soft, cozy throw across your lap. Put on a great book tape and relax while you stitch this colorful harvest piece. I used a variety of stitches, all very basic. Look at your favorite stitch directory and choose the ones you'd like to learn, then use them where they might be least expected. This could be a real learning project. You can put your gluing skills to good use in this project, too.

ITEMS TO GATHER

- General Items on page 10
- Wools:
  assorted scraps: browns; golds; greens; oranges
- Coordinating embroidery floss
- Micro-fiber yarn: bright yellow; coordinating with wools and polar fleece fabrics
- Polar fleece fabrics: lime green (2 yds); dark yellow (¼ yd); light yellow (¼ yd)
- Salad plate
- Threads: assorted; perle cotton

INSTRUCTIONS

Note: When stitching on fleece, remember that because of the fuzzy surface you can catch the surface of the fabric and not go though the cloth to the other side or you can treat it as a regular fabric, making the stitches go completely through the fabric to secure a more sturdy attachment for the pieces. The back side will, of course, show your stitches, but if you hide your starting knot under the edge of the piece you are appliquéing or through the fuzz of the fabric, you can keep the back looking neat. I used perle cotton, craft thread, and six strands of the embroidery floss. Oftentimes the choice of fiber I used was because of the color that I had available as much as anything else. I preferred the perle cotton, craft thread, and single twisted fibers to the embroidery floss.

1. Make certain that the fabric is evenly cut after washing, trim if necessary to square-up the fleece. Trim off the selvage edges.

2. Trim each corner so that it is rounded, using a salad plate as a pattern for the curve.

3. Finish edges of throw, using one of the following methods: (Photo 1)

   a. Clip the edges in to the fabric approximately 3"–4" deep and spaced up to 1" apart. *Note: The fringe can be left as is or tied into a simple knot for each piece of fringe.*

   b. Roll the edge and whipstitch, buttonhole-stitch, or machine-zigzag-stitch. Refer to Stitches to Know on pages 14–15.

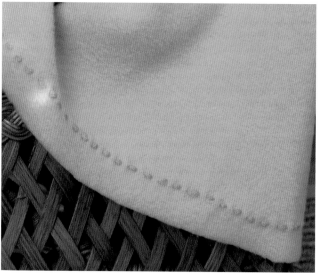

Photo 1

4. Photocopy Snugly Fall Blanket Patterns on page 119–120. *Note: If desired, patterns can be traced directly from book with tracing paper. Cut out as many flowers and leaves as desired from wool scraps. Note: Try varying the patterns in size and shape, so that nothing is exactly the same.*

Photo 2

5. Cut thin lengths of wool approximately ¼" wide for stems. *Note: Do not use a ruler, simply a straight scissor cut; that way they sort of ramble along and are not perfect.* (Photo 2)

6. Fold all circle patterns into fourths. Snip at each fold and unfold. Cut several times between those four cuts, creating flower petals. Round off each section, taper to a point, or add more cuts, removing some of the fabric between the cuts to create a fringe.

7. Lay the polar fleece out on the floor near where you are cutting and lay out each piece as you are cutting. *Note: This way, you can move things around adding and rearranging flowers and leaves, until you come up with an arrangement that is pleasing to you.*

8. Apply fabric glue to pieces, sparingly if hand-sewing or machine-sewing, or more heavily to firmly attach the flowers if you are not. (Photo 3)

Photo 3

9. Leave a few of the flower petals unattached to add dimension. *Note: If you do not like this look, you can always do more gluing or sewing after.* (Photo 4)

Photo 4

10. Stitch pieces onto polar fleece, using one of the following methods: (Photo 5)

a. If machine-sewing, choose matching or contrasting threads, metallic or shiny threads, or invisible thread. *Note: Remember the reverse side will be seen, so your bobbin thread could be the same color as the throw or an invisible thread.*

b. If hand-sewing, use embroidery floss and perle cotton. *Note: Because of the thickness of the materials, I chose not to use finer threads. Anchor pieces securely. There will be a lot of stretch.*

Photo 5

Variations:

Make a throw for each season. Make a different throw for each child, using different themes, shapes, and colors.

HOLIDAY CHAIR COVER

The variety of chairs is endless, so this pattern is very general and can be so easily adapted to fit your needs. It's a rectangular shape with ties to hold it in place. The ties can be moved about or you may want to make a pillowcase–like back with the sides sewn down. One thing to keep in mind: no one is comfortable sitting back on balls and garland. Keep the dimensional embellishments to the outside of the cover. The organza is added to make a slick surface so that the cover won't move as much while in use.

ITEMS TO GATHER

- General Items on page 10
- Wools:
  gold (¼ yd)
  white to fit chair measurement
- ¼"-wide silver acrylic stars
- Red metallic floss
- Satin plaid Christmas piping
  (4 yds)
- Threads: assorted; clear
- White organza 2" larger
  all around than chair
  measurement

HOLIDAY CHAIR COVER

INSTRUCTIONS

1. Determine how much of the chair you want covered, then measure the width and height of the chair. Cut the white wool to the size that best fits your chair.

2. Photocopy Holiday Chair Cover Patterns on page 124. *Note: If desired, patterns can be traced directly from book with tracing paper.* Cut four large stars and ten small stars from gold wool.

3. Glue large stars across one end of the rectangle for the back of the chair cover, lining up the horizontal arms on this edge with the tips touching each other. *Note: This will be the back side of the chair cover.* Glue the top half of each star in place. (Photo 1)

Photo 1

4. Scatter six small stars up the rectangle, noting where the wool will fold over the top and become the front side of the chair cover.

5. Place remaining small stars in a row across the top of the front of the cover, having the top points of the stars facing up toward the top of the chair. *Note: When folded over at the top, these stars should be about 2" down from that fold. Plan the placement of the stars around the horizontal "bars" of plaid piping, which will become the side ties. The piping will be added later.* Glue the small stars in place. (Photo 2)

Photo 2

6. Glue the small acrylic stars onto the white wool at each point of the four stars on the front side. Allow to dry.

7. Lay the chair cover on a flat surface. Place the organza over the cover. *Note: The organza should be larger on all sides.* Pin the organza in place in the center several times. Fold the sides and the starless edges back over the cover to the inside. Pin in place. The bottom star end of the piece is not covered with the organza. Pin the organza top fabric closely to the top edge of each star and trim excess organza that may cover the stars. Run a small bead of clear glue along this cut edge. Carefully tuck the organza under the top edge of the stars. Allow to dry. Glue the folded edges on the back into place or use a band of fusible interfacing and iron the edges into place, following the manufacturer's instructions.

8. Straight-stitch an outline on the top of the large stars with least three strands of the metallic red thread. Refer to Straight Stitch on page 15. *Note: This stitching is done on top of the organza.*

9. Straight-stitch an outline of each smaller star over the rest of the cover. *Note: The four stars in a row were only outlined on the top and bottom sides because each was joined by a small acrylic star.* Remove pins.

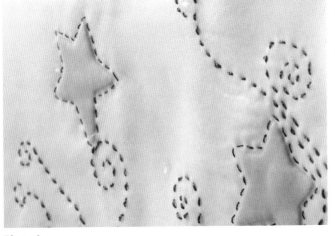

Photo 3

14. Place the piping across both sides of stars on bottom. (Photo 6)

Photo 6

10. Add swirls and curves as an accent between the stars with shiny green floss. Randomly, wind a curl around a small star to outline it. (Photo 3)

11. Cut piping into one-yard lengths. Place the cover on the chair and mark where the ties need to be placed. *Note: The piping must to be placed where it will best hold the cover securely.*

Photo 4

12. Attach the ties evenly so that you have the same "tail" length on each side. (Photo 4)

13. Shape the piping around the top of one small star to add contrast. (Photo 5)

15. Pin the piping in place, then sew it down, catching the underside of the cord from the wrong side of the wool with clear thread. Tack the ends of each cord down more securely where they end at each side of the wool.

16. Trim the cord ends to the desired length and knot each end. Add a dab of glue to the ends to prevent fraying.

Variations:

Attach bells or tassels to the chair covers. You can have names embroidered, or cut from colored wool, or made from a metallic cord. This simple design can be adapted for any season. You can add daisies, tulips, sunflowers, and autumn leaves. By lining the inside of the wool, you can also cut out a pattern from the wool and show the lining through to the front.

Photo 5

CHRISTMAS TREE SKIRT

This is a simple all-glue project. Turn on one of your favorite holiday movies, clear a place on the floor or on a big table, and have fun.

ITEMS TO GATHER

- General Items on page 10
- Wools:
  gold for stars (¼ yd)
  lavender rose for small ornaments (¼ yd)
  light blue for spirals (¼ yd)
  purple for large ornaments (¼ yd)
  scraps: green; deep rose; white; yellow
  white (1¼ yds)
- Christmas green shiny embroidery floss
- Threads: assorted; metallic silver thread
- Small hook and loop "dots" (6)

INSTRUCTIONS

1. Cut one 40" circle or desired size from the white wool. Fold the circle in half and cut on the fold into the center of the circle. Unfold and lay flat. Cut a smaller circle approximately 7" in diameter from the center of the large circle to accommodate the tree.

2. Enlarge Large Ornament Pattern 200% on page 122 and photocopy. Photocopy remaining Christmas Tree Skirt Patterns on pages 122–123. *Note: If desired, all patterns except the Large Ornament can be traced directly from book with tracing paper.*

3. Cut desired number of stars from the gold wool. Place stars around the edge of the skirt as desired. *Note: The tree skirt in this project has 30 stars. The stars were placed in a staggered pattern, then the white wool that extended beyond some of the stars was trimmed away, creating a ragged edge.* (Photo 1)

Photo 1

4. Cut desired number of large ornaments from purple wool. For each large ornament, cut three berries from deep rose wool and two leaves from green wool. Arrange leaves and berries onto large ornaments, creating holly berry ornaments. (Photo 2)

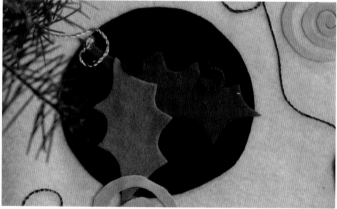

Photo 2

5. Cut desired number of small ornaments from lavender rose wool. Embellish each one with two thin strips of yellow felt and one white strip. When gluing the stripes down, curve them to match the curve of the ornament.

6. Cut out large and small spirals from light blue wool. Create spirals by cutting as shown on pattern. *Note: I found that I need to trim a little notch that is left as I*

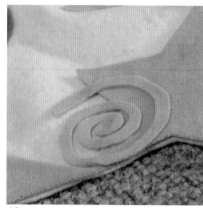

Photo 3

Photo 4

Photo 5

begin my spiral cut. I also go back in and trim off an edge of the spiral into the center to widen the gap of the cut so that the spiral is more open. (Photo 3)

7. Freehand-cut the snowflakes from the lavender felt. (Photo 4)

8. Arrange and manipulate pieces as desired on tree skirt. *Note: The design can be as uniform or spontaneous as you desire.*

9. When satisfied with the arrangement, carefully glue each piece onto tree skirt and press firmly to create a good bond. (Photo 5)

10. Place several strands of green floss around edge of center opening. (Photo 6) *Note: This serves two purposes, it strengthens and decorates the opening.*

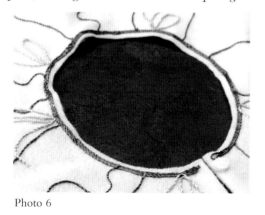

Photo 6

11. Curve and curl floss, creating a tendril effect down to a small ornament. Run a narrow length of clear glue down each piece of floss and carefully place down as

desired. Use pins to press the floss into the wool for a tight hold, if necessary. Repeat for each small ornament. *Note: This creates the look that the small ornaments are hanging from the tree skirt.* (Photo 7) Repeat with silver thread for holly berry ornaments.

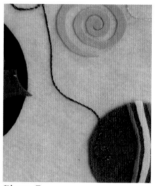

Photo 7

12. Fold each side of the tree skirt "back opening" under about ½", then glue. Use pins to hold these folds shut. *Note: A strip of iron-on interfacing can be used to close these folds.* Allow to dry.

13. Glue on the hook and loop "dots." Evenly space and place the fuzzy side of loop dots down one side. Glue the hook side to the matching side, aligned identically with the first dots. Carefully check skirt and make certain pieces are glued down securely. Use additional glue to secure, if necessary. Allow to dry. Recheck.

Variations:

Use different ornaments, colors, wool fabrics, metallics, etc., to decorate the tree skirt. Write your family's name or names around the edge, using a fine-tipped permanent-ink fabric marker or fabric paint. Glue lots of acrylic jewels to the skirt, use "eyelash" fabric to create a fun texture. Cut tiny openings to hold miniature lights from underneath the skirt.

WE THREE TREES

WE THREE TREES

ITEMS TO GATHER

- General Items on page 10
- Wools:
  3 different shades of green (½ yd each)
- 30" in length wooden molding in a rope design
- 20-gauge wires: blue; gold; red
- Acrylic Christmas lights: 1" bulbs (2 pkgs); miniature on a cord (1 strand)
- Acrylic paints: gold; silver; white
- Acrylic stars: ¼" (2 pkgs.); ½" (1 pkg.)
- Jingle bells: ¾" dia. (1 pkg.); 1½" dia. (2)
- Ribbons: ¼"-wide wire-edged silver metallic (1 bolt); ½"-wide silver tinsel metallic (1 bolt)
- Styrofoam cones: 9"; 12"; 18"
- White wire coat hangers (3)
- Wire cutters

INSTRUCTIONS

1. Photocopy We Three Trees Patterns on page 125. *Note: If desired, patterns can be traced directly from book with tracing paper.* Cut holly leaves, accent leaves and fringe from green wools.

2. Cover each Styrofoam cone in a different shade of green by pinning the straight edge of the wool down the seam line of the Styrofoam cone. *Note: Try to have at least 1½" of wool beyond the tip as you roll it.* Roll the cone with the wool until the pinned edge meets the uncut wool. Mark this line and add about ¼". Unroll the cone to the pins and mark a line on the wool again as you roll that follows the bottom line of the cone around, until it is covered with wool.

3. Cut the pattern you have just created and attach the wool to the cone with glue. Measure and cut a circle that is the same size as large end of each cone. Glue

in place. Pin the wool down the seam and at base where the side and bottom pieces meet to hold them together neatly. Allow to dry.

4. Using wire cutters, cut three lengths from hanger wire 3" longer than each tree height.

5. Make a loop at one end of each wire about ½"–¾" long. Cut a small slit in the center of tree base. Insert the straight end of each wire into each "tree" through the bottom. Place a dab of glue on the loop end, then push it slightly into the base of the tree. Make certain the straight end of wire comes out the top of the tree as close to the center as possible—a few tries will not hurt the project. When satisfied with the results, trim the top of the wire to approximately 1" above the cone. Carefully bend the wire end over to form a tight hook. *Note: The top of the wool that overlaps the end will hide the hook at the top and there will be a loop, showing slightly at the base.*

6. Cut various lengths from colored wire. Create spirals from the wires with ½"–¾" tails. Decorate the outside of each tree with spirals made from various wire colors. Insert the spiral tails into the cone in a downward position, then bend into desired shape.

7. On one tree, glue holly leaves around the spirals to secure the wires. Slip some of the leaves under or over the wires. Glue to secure. Glue individual plastic lightbulbs among the leaves. Glue fringe around the curve of each spiral on the next tree. Glue large acrylic stars as desired. (Photo 1)

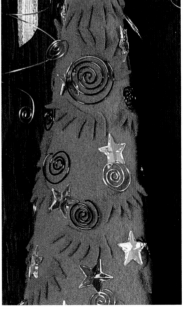
Photo 1

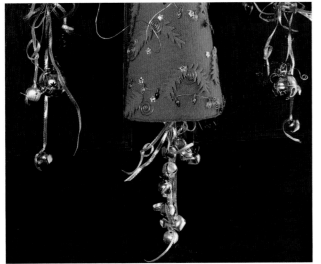

Photo 2

8. Glue the small stars and miniature strand bulbs individually to the third three. Glue accent leaves Pin into place until dry. Be careful removing the pins once the pieces are dry: twist a little back and forth on the stubborn pins and they should be easier to remove.

9. For the decorations at the base, thread ribbon through the partially exposed loop. Curl and swoop the small wire-edged ribbon around the loop. Thread some of the ribbons through the small bells and tie. *Note: These can hang at different lengths.*

10. Using colored wire, attach the large bells to the biggest tree and attach smaller bells to remaining trees. Attach curled wires to each tree's hook. Attach ribbon to the tree bottom by gluing and holding each one in place with a pin. (Photo 2)

11. While waiting for all the embellishments to dry, paint the rope molding. Base-coat the wood with a white paint. Allow to dry. Alternative every other twist with silver and gold paint. *Note: You can apply more than one coat of paint, depending on the brightness desired.* Allow to dry.

12. Carefully wrap remaining acrylic lightbulbs around and on the front of the painted molding. Use a clear glue to secure in place. Glue the light-bulbs to the wood wherever necessary, allowing some lights and cord to hang free. Allow to dry. *Note: You will want to let this dry very well.* Double-check any loose places and reglue.

13. From the top of each tree, thread desired wire through the hook, securing one end. Roll and curl all the wire before attaching the other end to the molding. *Note: The length of wire was determined by the length needed to make the trees hang at different heights.*

14. Attach each tree evenly spaced along the wooden molding. Attach a hanging ribbon to the two outside tree wires and tie into bows. Add some glue to hold in place. At the top of each tree, add additional curled wires, coming out the top in a mini celebration. Tie additional tinsel ribbon around the wool at the treetop. (Photo 3)

Photo 3

15. Wire the trees together in the back, from the center tree to each side tree, with curled wire. *Note: This will secure the trees in place and prevent them from rotating with the motion of the door.* Add the same curled wire to the outsides to carry out the design.

Variations:

What about striping each tree in red and white; gluing peppermint candies here and there, then having the candies spilling from the bottom of each tree held by wire and ribbon? You can paint the molding to look like a candy cane.

PATTERNS

THREE BIRDS PANEL PATTERNS

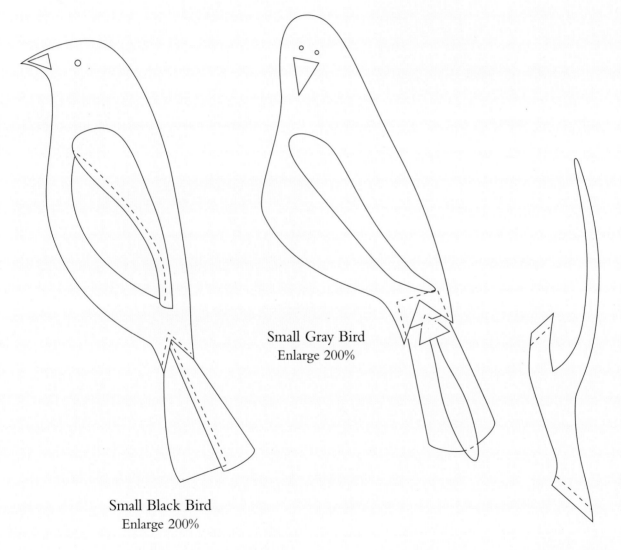

Small Black Bird
Enlarge 200%

Small Gray Bird
Enlarge 200%

Branch III
Enlarge 200%

THREE BIRDS PANEL PATTERNS

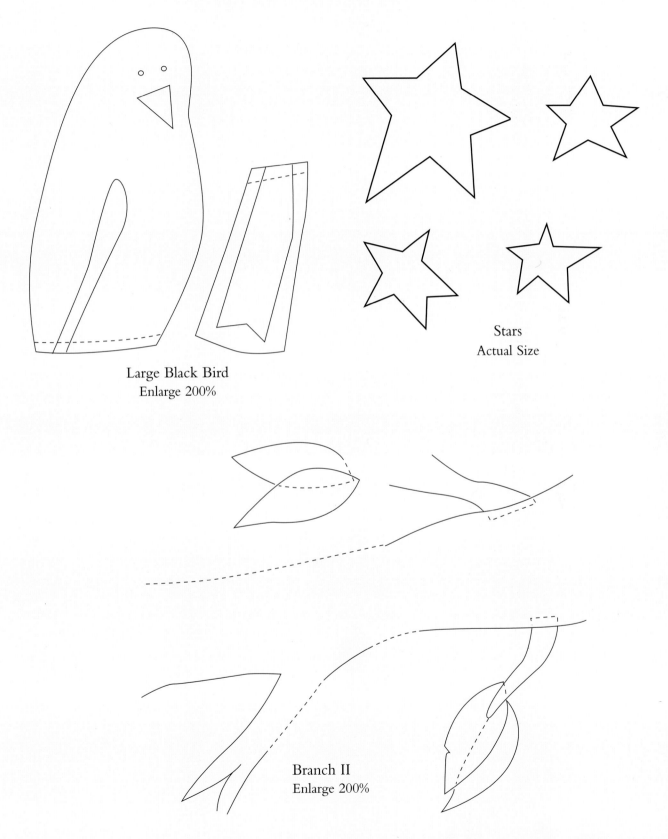

Large Black Bird
Enlarge 200%

Stars
Actual Size

Branch II
Enlarge 200%

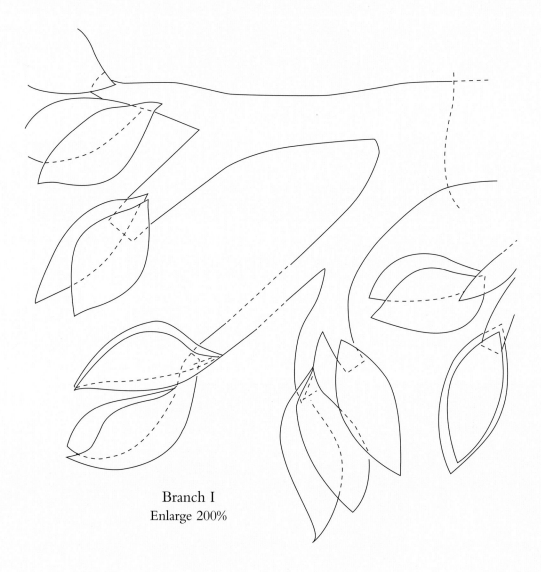

Branch I
Enlarge 200%

BIRDS WITH ATTITUDE PATTERNS

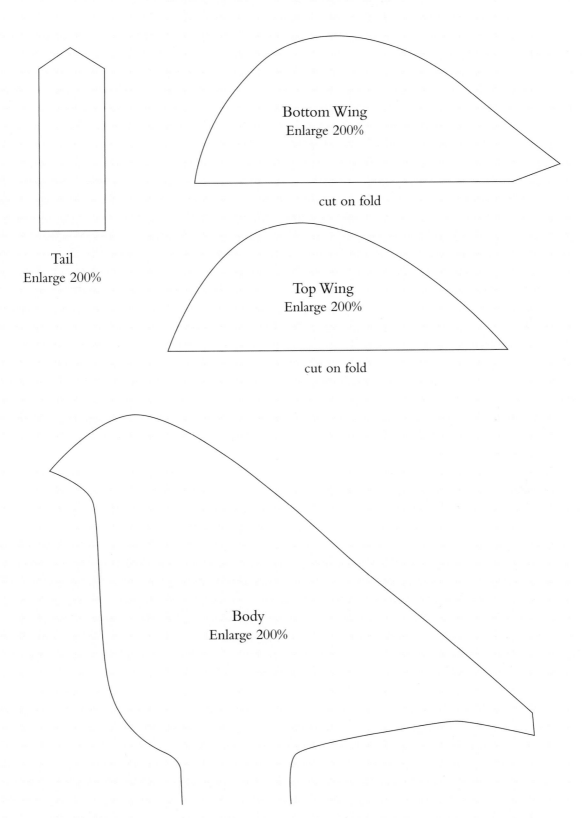

Tail
Enlarge 200%

Bottom Wing
Enlarge 200%

cut on fold

Top Wing
Enlarge 200%

cut on fold

Body
Enlarge 200%

BIRD PURSE PATTERNS

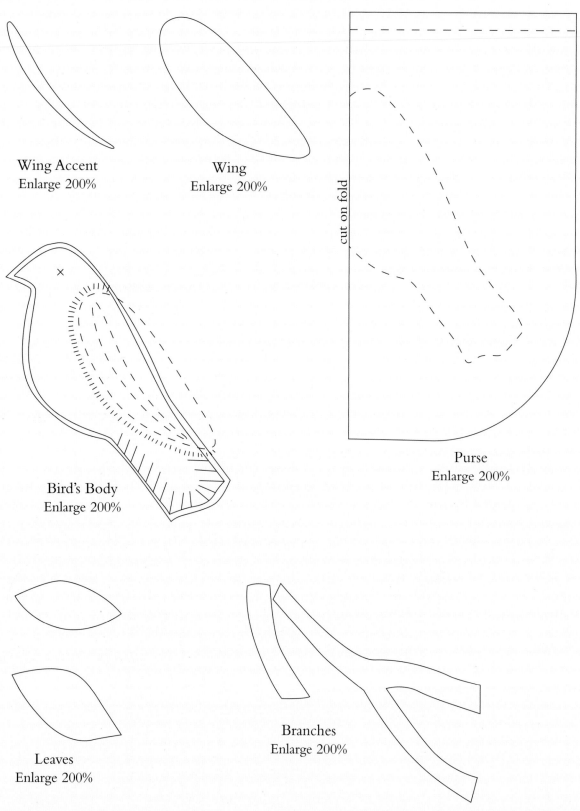

Wing Accent
Enlarge 200%

Wing
Enlarge 200%

cut on fold

Purse
Enlarge 200%

Bird's Body
Enlarge 200%

Leaves
Enlarge 200%

Branches
Enlarge 200%

FOUR-LEAF PANEL PATTERN

Leaf #1
Enlarge 200%

Leaf #2
Enlarge 200%

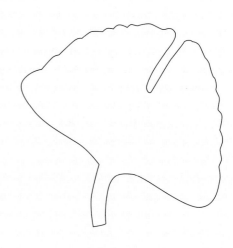

Ginkgo Leaf
Enlarge 200%

Leaf #3
Enlarge 200%

GINKGO TABLE RUNNER PATTERN

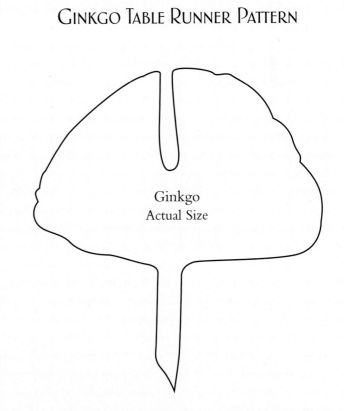

Ginkgo
Actual Size

Single Tree Panel Pattern

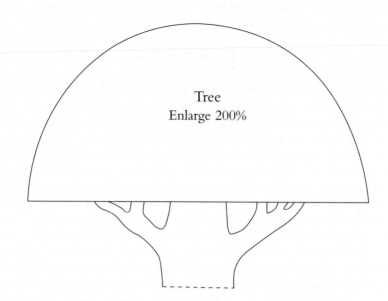

Tree
Enlarge 200%

Four Season's Wall Hanging Pattern

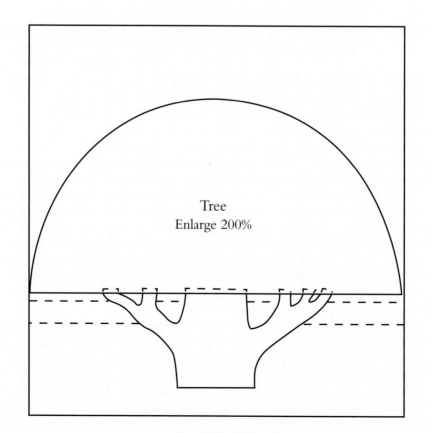

Tree
Enlarge 200%

THERE IS ONE IN EVERY CROWD AND FISH MOBILE PATTERN

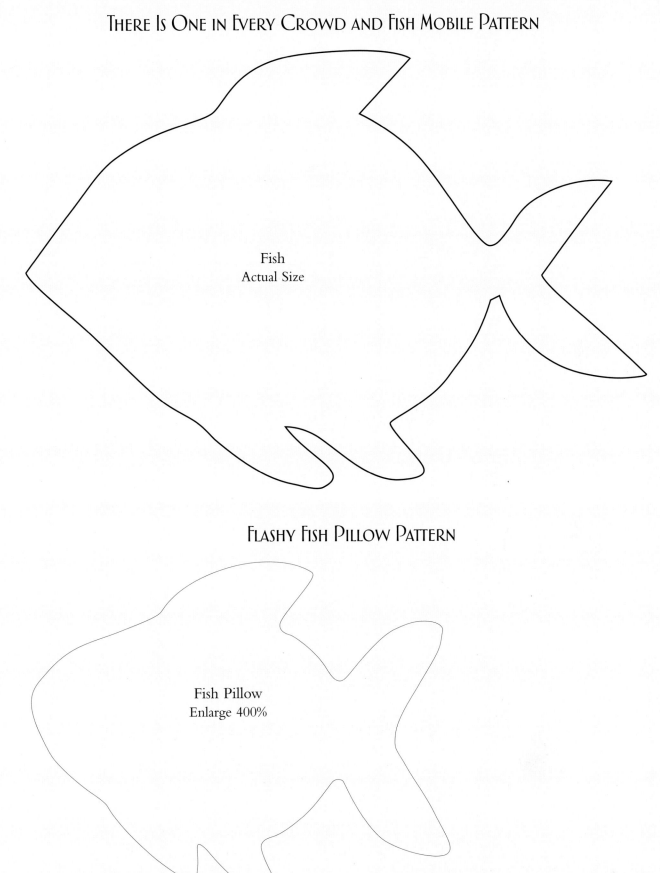

Fish
Actual Size

FLASHY FISH PILLOW PATTERN

Fish Pillow
Enlarge 400%

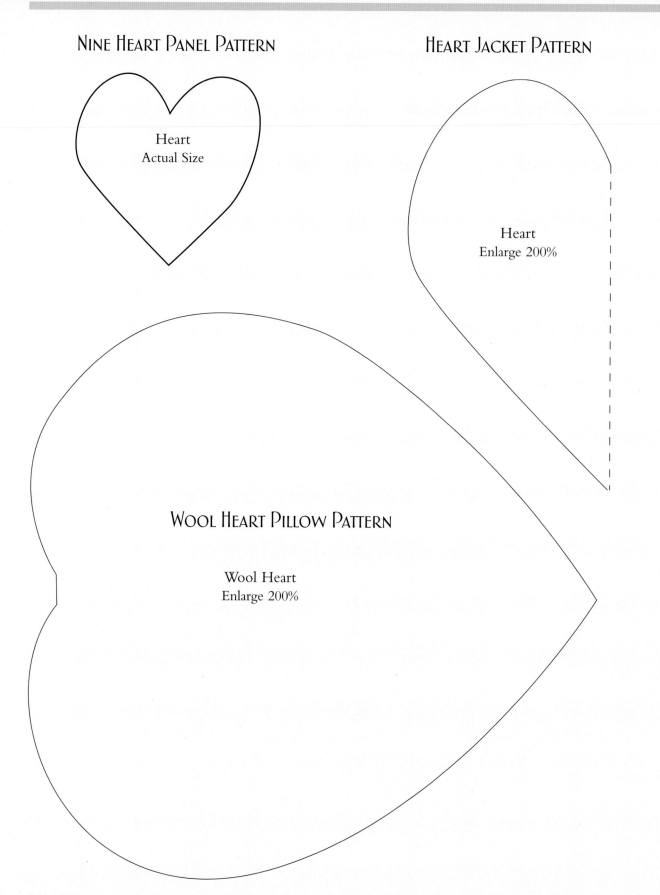

Nine Heart Panel Pattern

Heart
Actual Size

Heart Jacket Pattern

Heart
Enlarge 200%

Wool Heart Pillow Pattern

Wool Heart
Enlarge 200%

Cozy Foot Stool Patterns

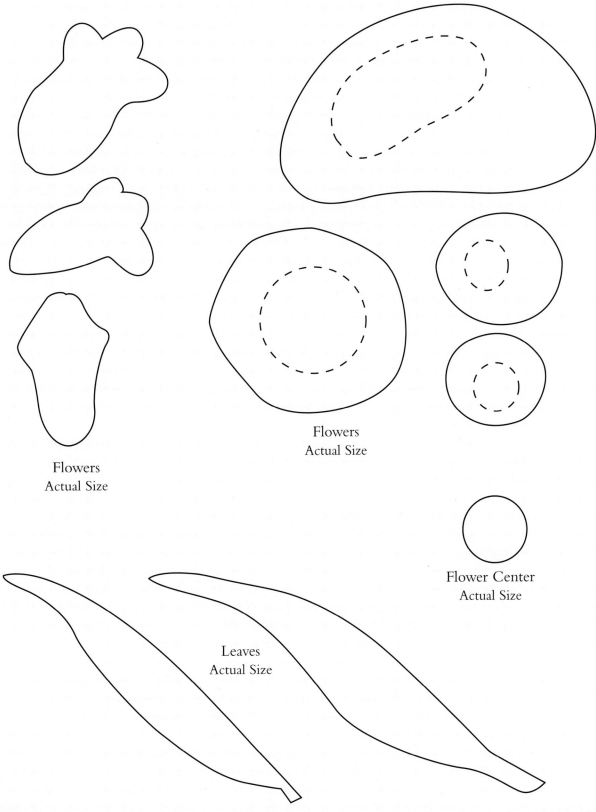

Flowers
Actual Size

Flowers
Actual Size

Flower Center
Actual Size

Leaves
Actual Size

Flowers
Actual Size

Flowers
Actual Size

Cozy Foot Stool Patterns

Snugly Fall Blanket Patterns

Leaves
Actual Size

Leaves
Actual Size

Flower Centers
Actual Size

Flower
Actual Size

SNUGLY FALL BLANKET PATTERNS

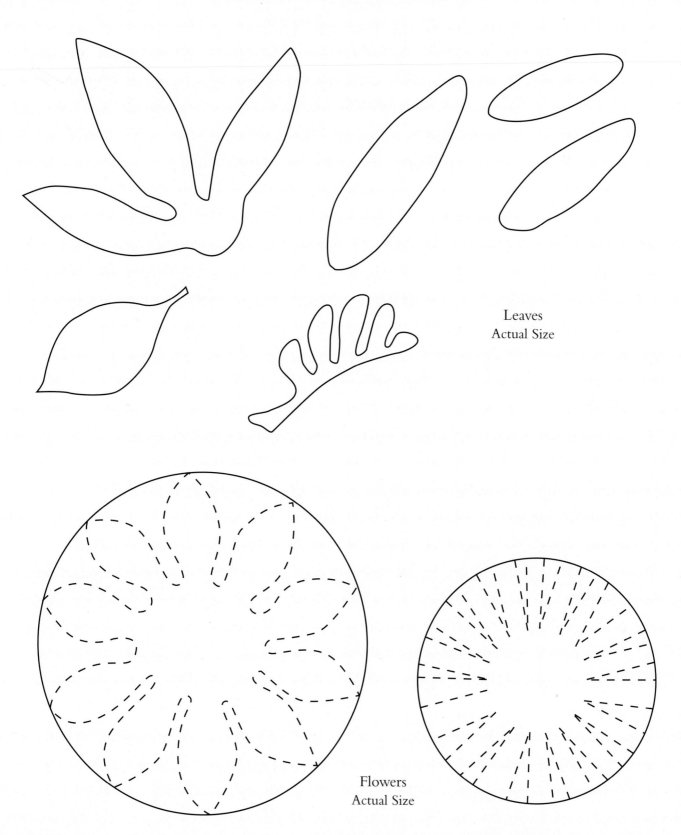

Leaves
Actual Size

Flowers
Actual Size

Spooky Wall Hanging Patterns

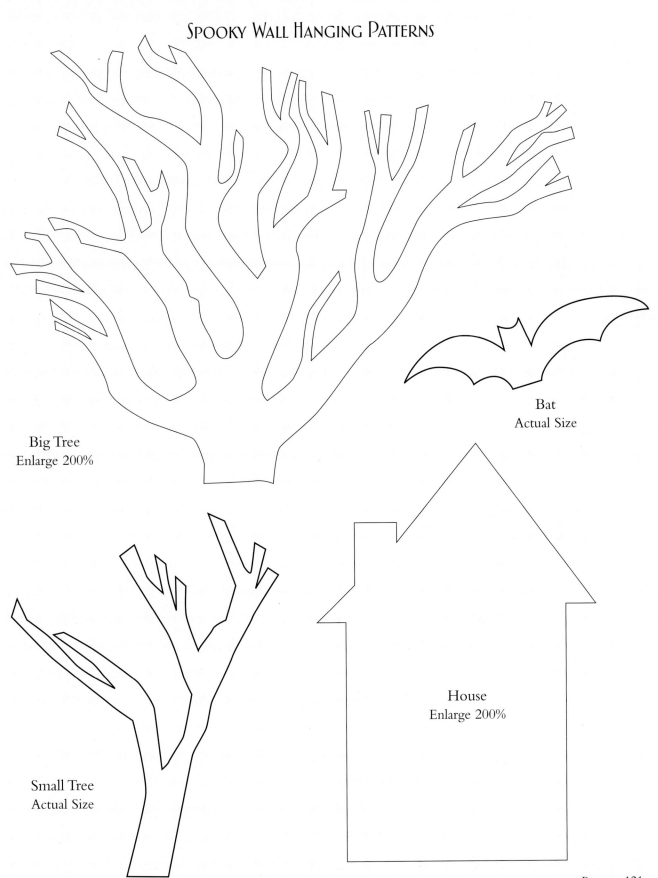

Big Tree
Enlarge 200%

Bat
Actual Size

Small Tree
Actual Size

House
Enlarge 200%

CHRISTMAS TREE SKIRT PATTERNS

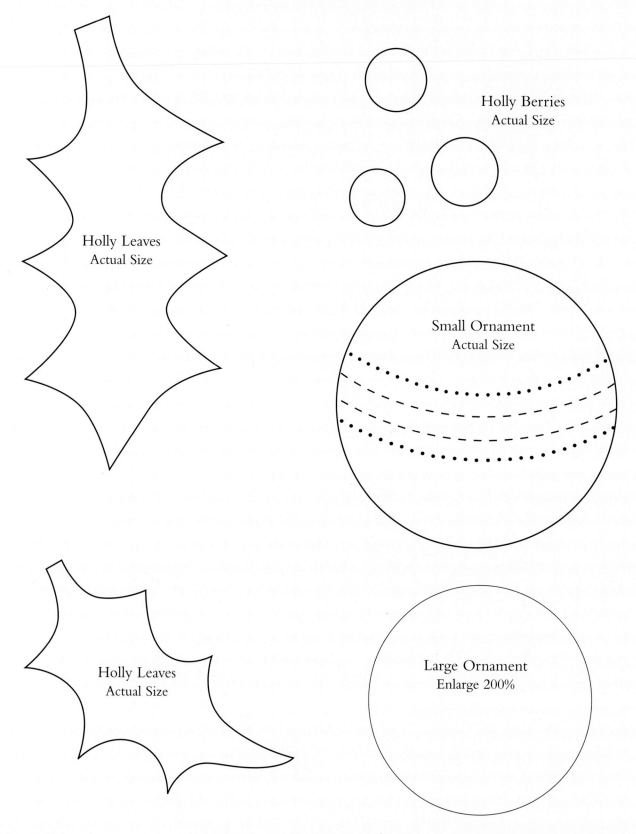

Holly Berries
Actual Size

Holly Leaves
Actual Size

Small Ornament
Actual Size

Holly Leaves
Actual Size

Large Ornament
Enlarge 200%

CHRISTMAS TREE SKIRT PATTERNS

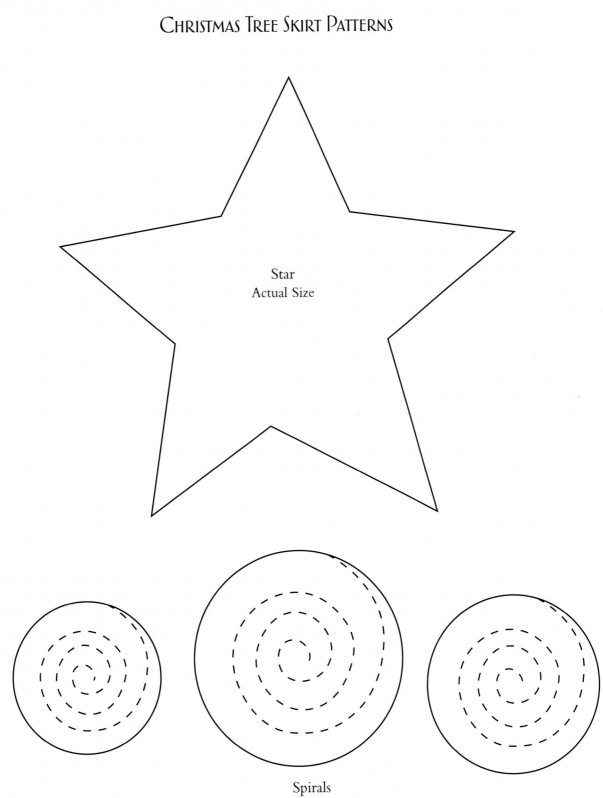

Star
Actual Size

Spirals
Actual Size

Holiday Chair Cover Patterns

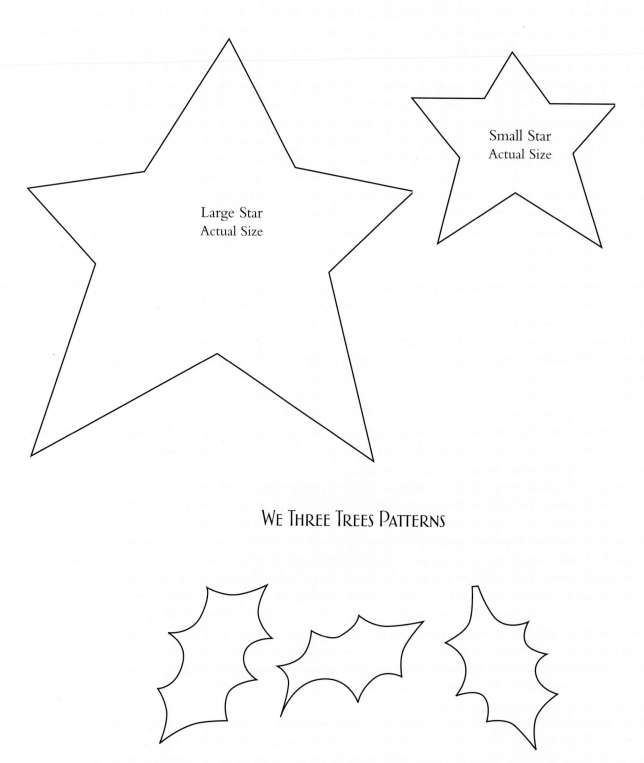

Large Star
Actual Size

Small Star
Actual Size

We Three Trees Patterns

Holly Leaves
Actual Size

WE THREE TREES PATTERNS

Fringe
Actual Size
Cut fringe where indicated by dots.

Accent Leaves
Actual Size

About the Author

SUSAN MCKEAN COTTRELL has always had a pencil or brush in her hand—ok, maybe a hammer, or a jar of glaze. She has fond memories of both her grandmothers teaching her at a very early age how to knit, draw, and to be creative. Her mother taught her to sew—what a wonderful world! She grew up in the midst of a large and creative family. Susan graduated from college with a degree in drawing and painting and has continued with both. She has contributed to Vanessa-Ann books and to *Crafts Magazine*, and has been involved illustrating a variety of how-to manuals and creating and setting up large instructional displays.

The most important individuals in her life are her husband, her four children, their spouses, and her wonderful and most delightful grandchildren. All have been everlastingly patient and supportive while being surrounded by paper, paint, ceramic dust, and yarn. Friends have added just what was needed to make her world very full.

Dedication

To the Giver of all things, I am truly blessed. To my dear family members, who are such a strength, and to my angel babies who fill my heart.

Acknowledgments

Thanks go to the wonderful individuals at Chapelle, Ltd. To Jo Packham and the long friendship and nudging, to Cindy Stoeckl and her patience, to Karmen Quinney and her magic. To all of the artisans at Chapelle, who most ably put polish to a rough stone. Thank-you to my good friends, who gave such wonderful encouragement and allowed me to believe that I could. What would I ever do without those nimble fingers?

METRIC CONVERSION CHARTS

mm–millimeters   cm–centimeters
INCHES TO MILLIMETERS AND CENTIMETERS

inches	mm	cm	inches	cm	inches	cm
⅛	3	0.3	9	22.9	30	76.2
¼	6	0.6	10	25.4	31	78.7
⅜	10	1.0	11	27.9	32	81.3
½	13	1.3	12	30.5	33	83.8
⅝	16	1.6	13	33.0	34	86.4
¾	19	1.9	14	35.6	35	88.9
⅞	22	2.2	15	38.1	36	91.4
1	25	2.5	16	40.6	37	94.0
1¼	32	3.2	17	43.2	38	96.5
1½	38	3.8	18	45.7	39	99.1
1¾	44	4.4	19	48.3	40	101.6
2	51	5.1	20	50.8	41	104.1
2½	64	6.4	21	53.3	42	106.7
3	76	7.6	22	55.9	43	109.2
3½	89	8.9	23	58.4	44	111.8
4	102	10.2	24	61.0	45	114.3
4½	114	11.4	25	63.5	46	116.8
5	127	12.7	26	66.0	47	119.4
6	152	15.2	27	68.6	48	121.9
7	178	17.8	28	71.1	49	124.5
8	203	20.3	29	73.7	50	127.0

YARDS TO METERS

yards	meters	yards	meters	yards	meters	yards	meters	yards	meters
⅛	0.11	2⅛	1.94	4⅛	3.77	6⅛	5.60	8⅛	7.43
¼	0.23	2¼	2.06	4¼	3.89	6¼	5.72	8¼	7.54
⅜	0.34	2⅜	2.17	4⅜	4.00	6⅜	5.83	8⅜	7.66
½	0.46	2½	2.29	4½	4.11	6½	5.94	8½	7.77
⅝	0.57	2⅝	2.40	4⅝	4.23	6⅝	6.06	8⅝	7.89
¾	0.69	2¾	2.51	4¾	4.34	6¾	6.17	8¾	8.00
⅞	0.80	2⅞	2.63	4⅞	4.46	6⅞	6.29	8⅞	8.12
1	0.91	3	2.74	5	4.57	7	6.40	9	8.23
1⅛	1.03	3⅛	2.86	5⅛	4.69	7⅛	6.52	9⅛	8.34
1¼	1.14	3¼	2.97	5¼	4.80	7¼	6.63	9¼	8.46
1⅜	1.26	3⅜	3.09	5⅜	4.91	7⅜	6.74	9⅜	8.57
1½	1.37	3½	3.20	5½	5.03	7½	6.86	9½	8.69
1⅝	1.49	3⅝	3.31	5⅝	5.14	7⅝	6.97	9⅝	8.80
1¾	1.60	3¾	3.43	5¾	5.26	7¾	7.09	9¾	8.92
1⅞	1.71	3⅞	3.54	5⅞	5.37	7⅞	7.20	9⅞	9.03

INDEX